HOW TO GET MORE OF YOUR STUDENTS INTO TOP UNIVERSITIES - from a state school.

John Hammond

HOW TO GET MORE OF YOUR STUDENTS INTO TOP UNIVERSITIES - from a state school.

ISBN 978-1-9164554-1-2

Copyright © 2018 J P Hammond

All rights reserved.

This book or any portion thereof may not be reproduced or used in any manner whatsoever without the express written permission of the publisher except for the use of brief quotations in a book review.

First Printing, 2018

10 Redwood Drive
Ferndown
Dorset
BH22 9UH

JOHN.HAMMOND20021955@gmail.com

Companion to the students' book:
"HOW TO THINK AND WORK SMART TO GET INTO A TOP UNIVERSITY - FROM A STATE SCHOOL."
By the same author, available as an eBook, or paperback, from Amazon.

Endorsements 1

Preface 3

1 Why read this book?... 5

2. What Private Schools do that your school might not. 13

3 How to organise yourself and your students to facilitate following the programme. 19

4. How to change your students' mind-set for success. 27

5. How to get them properly organised for study. 34

6. How to help them make the right A-level choice. 38

7. How to get to know your individual tutees. 41

8. How to ensure their Study Skills are REALLY effective. 46

9. What Study Groups are and how your tutees can use them to their advantage. 50

10. How to make sure they get the necessary grades. 52

11. Showing them how to maximise effective use of study periods. 69

12. Showing them how to make best use of genuine free time. 74

13. What they should do about paid employment. 78

14. How a healthy lifestyle affects the chances of success. 81

15. How to help them obtain work placements or internships that will improve their chances. 86

16. How to help them make the best University and degree choice. 89

17. The importance of making an early UCAS application. 93

18. How to help them write their best personal statement. 98

19. How to help them revise effectively, prepare well for exams and make best use of Past Papers. 107

20. What to do when their teacher is not up to the job. 112

21. How to help them when they feel low. 116

22. How to help them write really good essays. 119

23. How to help your students think about how to finance their degree. 123

Conclusion 128

Endorsements

Nicholas B, former tutee of the author.
As a successful former tutee of the author, I can guarantee that following the advice within these pages will help you on the path to achieving your future academic goals. Following the suggestions made with regards to organisation, general study skills, exams and UCAS will enable you to be independent and take control of your studies and your grades. This book also stands out for taking a holistic approach and considering issues which may seem insubstantial to your studies, but really are not (like keeping a healthy lifestyle). You CAN perform well and get into the university of your choice. I managed to get into one of the top law schools in the country despite the odds being against me because of my background (low socioeconomic status, first in the family to attend university). Being proactive and showing interest in reading this is a great first step.

Gideon King, former Director of Learning (Post 16)
Corfe Hills School
BH18 9BG
The challenges faced by young people as they move through GCSE and A level are multi-faceted and complex. The role of the school in providing academic and pastoral support is fundamental to their success, both in the medium and long term. I worked with John for over a decade at Corfe Hills School and knew him – first by reputation and later as a member of my team - to be someone who held fast to their belief that this support made a real difference to the outcomes and educational experiences of young people. By investing time, energy and care in his students - and more than a little challenge – John's approach to mentoring 'produced' students with confidence, independence and resilience; I know that many keep in touch with him to this day. John achieved what all of us in

education aspire to: he made a difference in the lives of young people. In crafting this book John has shared not only the essence but much of the detail of his approach. Educators and young people alike will find a wealth of information in here that is of practical value in their daily work.

Kathryn P, PPE Graduate, Oxford University, former tutee of the author.

If you are a student from any background interested in studying at a top university, this book offers a wealth of ideas to set you up for success. Reading this book has made me realise how many of these fundamental skills and strategies, built up during my GCSE and Sixth Form studies, prepared me brilliantly both for studying PPE at Oxford University and my career today. This book sets out a realistic approach to success in your studies, covering everything from how to use your tutors to what to do during your free time and even the importance of the right mental attitude and a healthy lifestyle. I would recommend any A-Level student determined to succeed give its ideas a try!

Preface

(A more detailed description of the scope of this book is to be found in the first chapter.)

This book is based on my knowledge and experience in helping ordinary students from an ordinary state school to achieve an extra-ordinary achievement. Namely to gain very good A-levels indeed and then a place at one of the highest ranked universities in the country.
I do not agree that money should buy anyone a better start in life, I believe that people should always be able to compete on a level playing field.

So years ago I set out to level that playing field.

By showing your students how to work smart, as well as hard, and with the inside knowledge of the ways private schools prepare their students via extra-curricular activities, which can be mirrored with your help, there is every reason to expect that you too will help them achieve greatness.

You will not find here some magic philosopher's stone that no one else knows about. None of what is here is psychobabble. All of it has been developed, tried, tested and perfected by myself and my students over a number of years. Their success stories are proof that it works.

By making minor changes to all you and they do while in the last two years before University, both inside school and, most importantly, out, you can make them add up to the major change needed to get your students ahead of where they would otherwise have been and indeed onto the podium of education winners, i.e. into a Russell Group university.

You do not need to be superhuman to put these skills into action. These guidelines are written for ordinary people. All you need to help them, is to persuade them to take a steady approach, to follow proven guidelines and to have faith that they are as good as anyone else who may seem better, but only because their parents can afford to send them to private school.

This will in fact make your job much easier. Once your charges get into the rhythm of working in this way, you will only need to keep an eye on them and help them with individual problems they may have.

I never needed to use time outside of normal registration time and this was run alongside, not instead of, the normal 6th form tutor programme.

I fervently hope that you will take on board the methods explained in this book and that you will help your students achieve the amazing success that they are capable of due to your, and their, efforts.

Best of luck!

1 Why read this book?

Who is this book for?
What is covered in the book.
Your students' mind-set.
How employers see results from top universities.
Graduate unemployment.
Helping them get things right.
My credentials and reasons for writing this book.

Who is this book for?

This book is principally aimed at sixth-form form teachers. Your title will vary from school to school, you may not even recognise the term "sixth-form" instead calling it "post 16" or "years 12 and 13", or some such. You may also be called "tutors" or "mentors". But basically you will be the person who sees a group of year 12 or 13 students every day, for registration, or goes with them to assembly etc. Your responsibilities will be pastoral, not subject based. (I will use the term "tutor" throughout to differentiate between your pastoral rôle and a subject teacher's rôle).

We are aware that caring parents, who cannot afford such a luxury, try their very hardest to make the state system work for them. They try to get their children into a grammar school, if one exists near them, or they move into the catchment area of a good state school. These may well be your students' parents or parent. If so this book will definitely help you. But if you are in the situation of working in a fairly ordinary state school, this book is even more for you.

I am very aware that this book may be read by a hugely differing range of people. From students at teacher training establishments to old hands who have been doing the job for decades. So you will appreciate that I have had to take this into account when deciding on a writing style.

I have had to tread a line between patronising those who know a lot about the job and going over the heads of those who are much newer to the environment. So I have gone for a very simple, practical and direct style. You will not find a high-brow treatise, full of theory, written in deathless prose. Everything will be very clear, down to earth and, I hope, concise. This does not mean that I will treat you as idiots, but I will always be bearing in mind the young teacher who has been put into the situation and is apprehensive about the responsibility he/she feels towards his/her charges.

Please try to be aware that I am writing this for staff who may not have the knowledge of some of the things that you feel should be obvious. So please be patient.

Also you may find my style very direct. I feel being direct cuts to the heart of the matter and is quicker in the long run. I am not going to be all wishy-washy when all it will do is result in vagueness and lack of success.

For all those who have a lot of experience then I accept that you may well skip quickly over what appears at first sight to be obvious. But the devil is in the detail and I would urge you to at least skim through the passage rather than completely ignore it. My time as a tutor enabled me to develop a whole load of little "wrinkles" that have made a difference that far outweighs the effort put in to master them.

What is covered in the book.

Unlike similar books you may find, this book covers building the metaphorical "house" of sixth-form studies and UCAS application from the foundations to the top of the chimney. It goes right back to the beginning of A-level studies, or even before, with the choice of A-levels.

It covers absolutely everything they need to do, from the first day of term, before classes, in classes, after classes, in "free periods", when revising, during exam preparation in all parts of life both in school and out, to absolutely maximise their chances of getting the grades and everything else they need.

Without them having to work like a demon, or to have an IQ of 140, the skills acquired within these pages, in simple, bite-sized chunks, will not only enable your students to get the best A-level grades but also to dot all the "i"s and cross all the "t"s essential to make a seriously good application via UCAS. This will also suit them for their degree studies, for further study and the world of work.

The point of this book is to help you show them how to compete successfully with the other students who go to private schools and how to mirror the activities they do and the advantages they have and even to beat them at their own game. Without it costing any money, other than the cost of this eBook. (And/or the students' book.)

Young people most emphatically DO NOT have to go to a private fee-paying school to ensure the best chance of getting into a Russell Group University.

This book is designed to help them bridge the gap between the two types of school as well as adding stuff on top that even private schools do not do.

There is much received wisdom about private schools that leads to state school students thinking they are somehow inferior or their school is inferior and frankly, most adults and even some teachers, think this way too, unfortunately. It is this mind-set that needs changing. They just need to find out how to focus their abilities and their efforts in the best possible way. To THINK and WORK SMART.

Your students' mind-set.

This book is aimed at helping you teach self-reliance. Explaining to them just what they need to do to get the best for themselves using the tools to hand and their own brains.

They will discover they will no longer have to rely on others, who may not be reliable.

They need to be told that if they believe that to be good, successful students all they need to do is to go to school and do what the teachers tell them, then they are wrong. That passive attitude may well get them reasonable A-levels and even into a reasonable university, but it will not get them to the top. This programme teaches them how to be proactive in their learning.

The information in this book is not some sort of magic bullet. It does not contain some amazing secret formula only known to me and Doctor Who. It DOES entail work. But only at the beginning. Once your charges have learned how to work smart, they will find they do still have time to enjoy themselves and have fun, they may even find they have _extra_ free time. This point needs emphasising. What it does contain is a mixture of forward thinking, organisation, planning, and skills that can only be learnt from someone who has been through the mill of helping students to make the best of themselves, over many years. I will not pull any punches. That said, I know that if you follow my advice and put into practice the methods I have used with my former students, you will gain success in getting them into the university of their choice or one of a similar status. They must however have the two basic requirements for success in anything, the will to achieve and the necessary basic intelligence.

Have a look at this - https://www.bbc.co.uk/news/education-42339106

to find some statistics about the lack of social mobility and how this is what your students will be overcoming.

I will show you how to organise your time with them in the most efficient way to facilitate your role as a tutor and to ensure that they will benefit to the max from the programme.

How employers see results from top universities.

At the moment (summer 2019) more than three quarters of all university students graduate with a 2.1 or a First. (https://www.bbc.com/news/education-48951653). The top employers therefore have difficulty choosing whom to employ, so they play safe. They take on graduates from the top universities.

Your students need to go to one of these to ensure a good job. Unless they decide to go for an apprenticeship of some kind or a fast-track approach. Whatever the future holds for higher education, there will always be competition for the best places. Everything in this book is aimed at helping you get your students to the top of the tree.

At the moment (summer 2017) three quarters of all university students graduate with a 2.1 or a First. (See Daily Telegraph article P12, 12/1/18 by Harry Yorke). I think we are all aware that this ludicrous situation means that the grades acquired are far less important than WHERE the graduate obtained his/her degree. Because employers can no longer use the grade of degree obtained by a graduate as an indicator of their employability, employers are looking for graduates from Russell Group universities, so they need to get into one. (This may all be rectified in the future by some national body being formed to oversee the validity of grades awarded. I do not feel this will be happening too soon and even if it does, the truth still holds that a degree from a top university is seen as better than one from another institution.)

This is important for another reason because students will continue to leave with enormous debt but a very good way of easing this problem by gaining well-paid employment is to have a degree from a Russell Group university, or a very specialised institution. If you are interested you could copy and paste this to see how much difference money makes.

https://www.bbc.co.uk/news/education-42401660 and

http://www.bbc.co.uk/news/education-41693230

Graduate unemployment.

Graduate unemployment has never been higher. Headline: "£50k less pay if you do the same degree at a lesser university." (Daily Mail June 14th 2017), referring to salaries being earned 5 years after graduation. Figures from the Department for Education.) Furthermore, in an article from the Daily Telegraph of the same date Dr Tim Bradshaw, director of the Russell Group, said "...the figures showed that employers were willing to pay a premium to hire graduates from top universities."

Especially in today's job market where competition for the best jobs is so tough, this is true for most graduates. Sorry to reiterate this but your students need to feel they owe it to themselves to get the best degree they can from the best university they can.

Helping them get things right.

A hard fact of life that no one may ever tell them, unless you do.

The powerful people who run big business and the country expect model job applicants, (and therefore model employees), to have got to a certain point in their qualifications by a certain point in their lives. They will not be bothered if a student takes a year off, or even does something like a short service commission in the forces, but they will be concerned if they do not fit into the recognised pattern of finishing A-levels and then going on to university quite quickly. If they have had to take a lot of time off to "find themselves" then they will be competing with all those who have not. So it pays them to get things right first time.

Conformity is boring and, you may well feel, as I do, unjustified, but it is a fact of life and they cannot beat these rich, powerful people. Even if they are lucky enough to find employers who are a bit more unconventional, then this bit of advice will not hurt them.

This book will enable you to help them to get all this right first time.

My credentials and reasons for writing this book.

Year after year, despite the school I taught in being just a provincial comprehensive school, my students ended up gaining places that they, or their parents, would never have thought possible. Gaining A* grade A levels instead of just Bs and Cs and offers from Russell Group universities. And you will learn what I did.

I personally went to a Public HMC school then I went on to teach in a normal state school. Obviously I know a thing or two about what the private schools do and I therefore know how to help students in state schools compete with them.

As far as my credentials are concerned, (skip this bit if you wish!) I taught for nearly 34 years in a 13 to 18 mixed comprehensive in the south of England in a place where ordinary schools had to compete with Grammar Schools and Private Schools. Inevitably, my school was thus "creamed". The brightest students in the area usually passed the eleven plus and went to the grammars, so our students consisted mostly of the normal school population minus the top 20% or so. You would have thought that we would have been lucky to get many students into university, never mind the Russell Group. However, students from my tutor group managed to get into Oxbridge and the Russell group universities, quite a few from families where no other family member had ever been to university. I managed to have students who scored three A* at A level. Generally my tutees were the first to achieve important tasks, like getting their UCAS applications in early. They also won prizes as a group when competing against the rest of the year group. This was noticed by the school's senior staff and they decided to give me a tutor group called the "Elite" tutor group. This consisted of students who were bright, possibly, but, above all, hard-working, determined and open to fresh ideas. Or else ones who needed special attention. Thus I was able to ensure that they all had the chance to follow my advice and do as well as they possibly could in the last two years of school, finishing by going on to the university of their choice, to do the course of their choice, or by going into the job they wanted to do. They keep in touch and they have urged me to write this book. Why do I bother? I have retired and spend half my life in France. I do not expect to make much money from doing this. I am doing it because I think it is unfair that students whose parents have a lot of money should benefit from a better education. I am an egalitarian and I feel all people should have an equal chance in life, or at least as fair a chance as is possible. So in this unfair world I am just trying to tip the balance a bit towards the side of the not-so-privileged.

Best of luck and "Here goes"

2. What Private Schools do that your school might not.

You may have only a vague idea of what is different about being educated in a Private School. If you went to one, or taught in one, then this chapter may well seem a waste of your time, but I think it might be an idea just to skim through it, if this is you, as there may well be insights into what goes on in one, that never struck you as important but that it is still a good idea to impart to your youngsters.

It might be edifying, and will cost you nothing, to send off for a couple of Sixth Form Prospectuses from Public (HMC) schools.

I find that although they are quite specific and do cover a lot of the ground that I cover in this book, *they still do not do all the things that my tutees did* in order to achieve their full potential. The tricks that they miss, you will not miss as they are to be found further on here.

In this chapter I am going to explain what it is private schools do and how you and your students can get around it. In fact I am going to give you, and them, advantages in the mind-set needed to succeed that not even private schools give their students. The difference being that I will be very direct and clear about what needs to be done rather than doing what many private schools do which is kind of relying on a sort of osmosis happening. Just being in school, even the best of private schools, is not enough to guarantee success.

You may wish to clarify to your students that a Public School is a private fee-paying school that is a member of the Head Masters' and Headmistresses' Conference. And that not all private schools are in the HMC, but even the worse private school still gives its students advantages. (If they are really bothered, they can always search for HMC on the internet. But the term Public School is certainly confusing for some students.)

On August 15, 2010 "The Observer" reported that the gap between the A-Level achievement at private schools and that at state schools in the UK was set to widen, with three times as many privately educated students achieving the new grade A*. The paper also noted that, according to the Fair Access Watchdog, bright students from the poorest backgrounds are seven times less likely to go to a top university than their richer peers.

This has not changed much in recent years. So how do they do this?

Firstly, the parents who send their kids to private schools have to be prepared to spend money on their education. Here we are talking huge sums of money. The average Public School charges parents about £30k per year, if their child "boards". (You may need to explain this term.) Those who do, benefit to the max from the school environment. So it costs about half a doctor's take-home pay to send one child to private school.

Why is this important? Well, you can imagine the emotional blackmail, the pressure that a parent can bring to bear on a child when they are spending that amount of money on them. Unless the kid really hates his mum and/or dad, they will be aware of this and will try hard to respond by working well at school.

In a state school, students are not under that pressure. Education is free, to all intents and purposes. Parents pay the council tax and expect their little ones to be educated well. OFSTED is there to ensure that school does its job properly and that's it, isn't it?

Well, I'm sure you would agree that if that was all it took, few people would spend all that money on getting the job done privately.

Secondly, a private school has a whole different lifestyle and environment to that of a state school. Most private schools are selective, i.e. you have to pass an exam to get into them. Most commonly, and for all the best HMC schools, this exam will be Common Entrance, taken at 13 years of age. But the students in private schools have mostly been educated privately all their school lives, so the private school ethos is well and truly ingrained in them by the time they get to the sixth form.

Once you cross the threshold you arrive almost on another planet. Once the parents have handed over the money, they then hand over the child. The school takes the child over and that student then becomes part of the whole private school ethos. All parts of this are designed to ensure the child not only succeeds academically but also in other ways. This means that said student not only leaves the school to go onto a glittering academic career, if that is what they want, but also to a place in society, a social elite, where they will almost automatically obtain a career and a lifestyle that will perpetuate the private schools as being the "go to" place for success.

This is where state schools generally do not and cannot compete, and where you can level the playing field.

Private schools need to do this to ensure they stay afloat. Many private school students then go on to send their own children to the same school. So they DO work.

Once in a private school, life becomes a series of events that are timed and programmed by the school. If you board, you get up at the same time, go to breakfast in the same place, and wear the same uniform from the time you get up until the time you go to bed, more or less. Uniformity becomes second nature.

But this is not just to do with time and place, it is subtly and subconsciously to do with how the students think and work. All is designed to get them used to behaving in a way that has been proven to be successful. They may only be allowed off the premises at certain times, for instance. Evenings and other times a state school student thinks of as being "his/her personal time", in a private school is taken over, controlled by the school.

"Prep" for instance. Supervised "homework". (I put this in speech marks because the students are not at home.) In the state system, you give homework. The students do it, or they don't, whenever is convenient to them. At private school, they have no choice, they do it and they DO do it, and if they board, they do it when the school decides. It is supervised. Not doing it is not an option. There are no excuses, there is nowhere to hide.

They are strongly encouraged, almost made to take part in other activities which are open to them, not just incredible amounts of sport or other team games, which keep them fit and healthy, whether they want it or not, but all sorts of societies, debating groups, Bridge clubs and others, musical opportunities, cadet forces, etc.

Through the prefectural system, many if not most students are given responsibility for younger students. They become managers.

These are all designed to allow the students to enjoy themselves, to build team spirit, competitiveness and the ability to manage others. Thus equipping them for life in high powered jobs in industry, the City, the forces, the Law, Medicine or elsewhere.

The forms of control that private schools exert and which make the students work hard and achieve well, cannot be done in state schools, this is why your students need to realise their existence and to understand that through exerting self-control, they can emulate this system and thus perform as well as, if not better, than private school students.

Also it is FAR easier to expel a student from a private school. For instance, times have possibly changed, but in my school all you had to do to "get the sack" was to be caught smoking 3 times. So it puts pressure on the pupils to toe the line in a way that a state school cannot.

Throughout the other chapters I will be explaining in much more detail the steps you can take which will negate the advantages that private schools have and give your students the same if not better chances than they have.

Some things you will not be able to change. For instance - small classes. I was regularly in classes of six to ten students, never more than twenty. In some cases private school students will be in classes of one or two students, so they get more or less one-on-one education. You know, but maybe your students don't, that not many state institutions can afford this luxury. Normally in a state school, if a class is not big enough to justify its existence then the class will not be allowed to run and I do know of whole departments being shut down because not enough students wanted to do the course. In private schools the parents pay for their kids to do the course they want and by and large this happens. But by using proper study skills this advantage can be largely overcome.

What sort of teacher decides to teach in a private school? Or is employed in one? This may well be a sensitive topic for you! But in my experience they are generally well-qualified. Although many of them just do not have the stomach to teach in a state school with all the rough and tumble that entails. It may need to be explained to your students that the competition for such easy teaching jobs is quite tough; contrasting that with the difficulties state schools endure trying to recruit. Almost all the teachers in my school had degrees from Oxbridge. Many had very good links with their old colleges which doubtless helped with applications to those colleges. I personally met my chemistry teacher's Don from Cambridge.

Private school teachers have different responsibilities to their colleagues in state schools, their hours and holidays are different and they normally have to be prepared to run sports and/or some other form of extracurricular activity. They do not have the same ethos as state school teachers a lot of the time. But then they do not have to put up with students who do not want to behave. (Students who misbehave regularly, do not last five minutes in a private school.) So you have clever teachers teaching well-behaved, small classes. Is it any wonder these students do well?

The schools also have more money to spend on the latest equipment, books, computers, etc. Far more than state schools. So, this should give your students an idea of what they are up against, what the parents are buying for their money and what they have to think about if they want to succeed at least as well as private school students do.

But the whole point of this book is to help you to make them realise that, provided they are prepared to make an effort to follow the sort of regime that I will show you, they will no longer be at such a disadvantage and they will achieve the same level of success that private school students enjoy, without someone having to pay such huge fees.

3 How to organise yourself and your students to facilitate following the programme.

Groups

Registration and Attendance

Information exchange

Paperwork

Timing

Place

Other events

If you do not have registration.

Do not be at all worried about this. The last thing I ever wanted to do as a teacher was to work any harder than I already was doing!

I am not some kind of fanatic workaholic and you will not need to bust a gut to get your students to follow this programme.

Once you have read this book through, what you will be doing with your students will fall into place, but here you will find a way of organising groups, time, paperwork and events.

Groups

Firstly tell your students what they are going to be doing, in broad brushstrokes and get them organised into small friendship groups. How many are in each group will vary according to how much time you have with them at registration, or whatever. But most schools tend to have about 20 minutes for registration.

Right at the beginning it is made clear to the whole group that they would be working, about once a fortnight, in a small group. I encourage friendship groups because students feel more relaxed like that and are very much more likely to help each other out.

Inevitably, there will probably be a group of "left-overs" who simply do not have any friends in the tutor group, so do not make up part of a friendship group. I found that this group that was accidentally formed, did in fact gel. I offer no explanation as to why this should be. At the first couple of sessions they were quite quiet but very soon they relaxed and worked just as well as the other groups.

Sixth form college tutors are more likely to have this sort of subgroup, but nevertheless, they will still prefer working in a group than one-on-one with you. Sad but true!

Each of my groups was just given a letter, A,B,C, etc. But if you wish to let them come up with some trendy name for themselves, it is your choice. I preferred to make it clear that they would be doing a job of work, which I would be taking very seriously and that I expected them to do the same. It didn't mean that there would not be any laughs along the way, there were, quite often, as that is my personality, but the whole point of the group work is to instil in them the idea that for 15 minutes, every two weeks, they will be prepared, receptive and ready to be put on the spot.

Registration and attendance

This time is usually seen as a complete or near complete waste of time by the students, once they get over the shock of being in the 6th form. So you have to grab them right at the start, when they are still coming to registration!

As you sow so shall ye reap. Make it extremely clear to them that missing registration is not an option. If students do miss it, use your school's system to find them later on in the day, (most schools have a SIMS system or similar, which makes this a piece of cake), hoick them out of class and ask them why they missed registration. How you take it from then on is up to you, but I found that a bit of tough love was all it took.

Information exchange

I suggest making it very clear to them right from the beginning that the information-giving part of reg. is going to be a formality, important and not to be missed, but nevertheless a quick, formal sharing of information. They will not be kept ages listening to interminable reading out of lists of events etc. Also take this opportunity to get all their email addresses and put them into a group. This is vital if an opportunity comes along that they might be interested in. You can simply send them a group email and they can respond as they see fit.

Of course your school or college may already be making you do this...

Hopefully they do not see this as an infringement of their personal space. If so maybe you can set up a site they have to visit once a day. I would not advise setting up a Facebook group, the reasons should be obvious.

When you go 6th form office every morning, get any necessary info and then write it up on the white board, in your form room. Or it could be projected from a lap-top. Thus the students come in, sit down, get their diaries out and note anything of importance. No excuse for not having it, i.e. being late could not be a reason.

Individual notes and other paperwork for individual students you simply place on their tables (They are creatures of habit and always sit in the same place.)

This being done before they come in, apart from actually calling the register, the rest of the time can be used as follows.

If part of the programme needs to be worked on as a tutor group then use that time for that, but if working with one of the smaller groups, make the rest free to go or stay, Let them choose, treat them like adults, they will appreciate it. Unless of course the school can justify keeping them in their tutor base.

Students aren't stupid, they rapidly see that they will be treated with respect and their time will not be wasted.

But right at the very beginning it is made clear to them that they have to come on time, be properly equipped and in proper uniform or dressed in line with the dress code. Obviously the latter will vary from institution to institution, but make it clear to them that getting used to being properly dressed means getting used to being smart and comfortable in such clothes. This being important because they will probably be trying, in future, to work in a company at a high level. If wearing such clothes is second nature to them, they will be far more confident and therefore likely to impress effortlessly.

Again, sending students home to change into something more suitable is something that only has to be done once usually. (This is assuming that you get back-up from the year staff.)

Properly equipped for me means with a diary and a writing implement.

Paperwork.

One way of doing this which is easy and quick. I simply had a loose leaf binder in which all my info on the tutor group was kept.

Each A4 page was headed with the letter for the friendship group, and on each page there was a space for each student. I printed up proforma for these to save time. For each student there was space for their name, the date, action taken since last meeting, agreed action to be taken and a time bracket for the action to be achieved in, e.g., "By next meeting". So 5 students per page, it could have been 6 and if you write big, or lots, you could use both sides of the paper!

Students will know that at the time of the next meeting, this piece of paper will be produced and the record will show what each student was supposed to have done. They bring their diaries to the sessions, note action to be taken, date, time period, etc. so their record matches yours.

It is thus absolutely clear to them that you know exactly what is going on at all times and if they slip backwards then you will take action.

This sounds more threatening than it is. With my students, after a chat and a chance to explain to the group what had caused the delay, we agreed on fair action and usually they helped each other. A simple extension was usually all it took.

I am sure you will find this works for you.

Timing.

As you have probably gathered, in my case, each of these sessions took place during a registration period. Now if your school is like mine there is a good chance that you will have Assembly once a week and Tutor Period, (or whatever it is called in your school), once a week as well. This leaves you 3 registrations. Now the maths is fairly easy, if you have 20 tutees and you form these into 4 groups of 5, you will be able to see each group easily once a fortnight, in fact more often on a rolling basis, should you choose. If you have 30 tutees then you will have 6 groups, which you will still be able to see once a fortnight each. Provided you are prompt and students know exactly which group will be seen each day, then, by being business-like, it is quite possible to deal with 5 students in one session of 15 minutes. I know that you, as my colleagues did, may find this hard to believe, but my students all did it and the results speak for themselves. Bear in mind that the conversation with each individual student was likely to be the same as with all the others so they could see what was coming and it went really fast. But if 5 really is a problem for you, you could make it 5 groups of 4 and just see them a fraction less often.

If you contrast this with the idea of tutoring each tutee individually, the maths makes it obvious that with only 3 opportunities a week, it will take 10 weeks to get around the whole tutor group. You will only see each individual about 3 times in a year before exams start. This is pretty well useless. And furthermore, 15 minutes is a long time to spend discussing with just one student. Even if you see them rarely, everything that needs to be said gets said in the first few minutes. Also, if they don't want to see you, all they have to do is take the appropriate day off.

Some sixth-form colleges have two-hour sessions with their groups. Poor things, I bet the students dread them! "Little and often" is the key to most skills and what we are dealing with here is a set of skills.

I think you would be unfortunate to have as many as 30 tutees, so you will probably find that you can see each group on a rolling basis more often than once a fortnight, or you could do what I did which was to leave Fridays open so the students had nothing special and we could just chat or they could bring individual problems to me.

Anyway, these sessions become far less intense very quickly and are replaced with other stuff which I will mention in a minute.

Place.

I was very lucky in that I had a small room off my tutor base, which I could use for these sessions, but honestly it isn't necessary, and you can simply take the group to a corner of the tutor room. If you have been able to free the others to go, there will always be enough room.

The important thing to do is to get them into the habit of being organised and working as a team. The team spirit that all this engenders I am sure is worth a grade or so at A level, purely as a result.

What was always noticeable to me was how soon it became obvious that my tutor group were all attending registration when other tutor groups apparently got smaller and smaller. In my school we had to walk through each other's rooms and I often saw groups with only a handful of tutees there.

More on the importance of simply turning up, later.

Other events

Once the first few weeks' activities have passed, you will find yourself needing to use the time available to address the group as a whole on various topics within the programme. You will also want to be guiding them towards making presentations, getting the rest of the group to comment on these, getting the groups to do practice interviews with each other and many other things that you are probably doing already. I am well aware that all of you will have things that you know need to be done and may well be part of a sixth form programme that you have to follow, but you will see how well these meld in with the programme as you go along.

From now on, when each chapter covers what you will be doing I will cover the admin side when it is not obvious.

If you do not have registration.

If you are a personal tutor in a sixth form college then registration is unlikely to be something that is part of the day. However, you will still meet with your students on a regular basis. I suggest you read through what comes next and decide how you can apply this to your timetabled meetings with your students.

If you meet with the group once a week for an hour that is actually longer, i.e. more contact time, than they would get in an ordinary school. So you can address the group as a whole, divide them up into sub-groups and set them all targets, then you can continue to see them in their subgroups on a fortnightly basis.

If the powers that be dictate to you how you spend your time with your tutees then you will need to think outside the box. If you foresee hassle then it might be easiest to suggest to your students that they buy the student version of this book, "How to think and work smart to get into a top university – from a state school." which is available very cheaply, from Amazon, either as an eBook or paperback. But if you think your management might be a bit more open-minded then you could try asking them to give the tutor system a bit of a rethink to accommodate the ideas which you know will work.

I am not being big-headed, I am very confident that you will see the wisdom of tutoring like this once you have read this book. If your bosses read it, they will see the stuff contained within it is sensible, down-to-earth and will only require a minimum shift in emphasis to gain a much bigger result.

As I keep saying, it runs alongside any tutor program and frankly puts the mortar between the bricks of that program.

4. How to change your students' mind-set for success.

(What theirs should be and understanding those of their teachers.)

Your students may be on the following, not exhaustive, list.

Teenagers. Who know it all. Their parents are boring people who only want to preach and find fault with everything they do.

They are lucky, their parents love them to bits and cannot do enough for them, they know they don't know it all and they do everything you and their parents say without question.

They think they are streetwise, ahead of the curve, winners, movers, shakers.

Add your own categories to this list, I have found many more!

They need it explaining to them that, whoever they are, it is a medical fact that their brains will not be fully developed until they are about 25. So they will need help with their mental attitude towards study.

> (Isabelle Chaffai – Psychotherapist) "It may seem logical that those aged 18 to 25 are completely mature, in fact the brain still is maturing – specifically the area known as the "prefrontal cortex." Changes occurring between ages 18 and 25 are essentially a continued process of brain development that started during puberty. When you're 18, you're roughly halfway through the entire stage of development. The prefrontal cortex doesn't have nearly the functional capacity at age 18 as it does at 25. This means that some people may have major struggles with impulsive decisions and planning behaviour to reach a goal. The brain's reward system tends to reach a

high level of activation during puberty and then gradually drifts back to normal activation when a person reaches roughly the age of 25. Adults over the age of 25 tend to feel less sensitive to the influence of peer pressure and have a much easier time handling it."

(You will find a slightly different quote on this in the chapter on "Healthy Lifestyle").

Why am I quoting this? Because it is important for your charges to realise that, mature though they may feel they are, they still need input from experts to ensure they are helped to make the right decisions.

This is of course one of the hardest things to get across to adolescents.

I found that depersonalising this, getting students to do some research and finding what scientists and social psychologists have found, gets them away from thinking "Sir/Miss is such an old fogey, always banging on about how we all need to listen to older people."

Their parents, bless'em, are often too close to them to be able to be objective. (If they care and can see beyond their dress, choice of friends and how much noise they make with their music, that is!)

Their friends are no more experienced than they are, but unfortunately certain of their more charismatic peers can have an untold, deleterious effect on their thinking, but more about how to get around this later. (Later on you'll read how in fact they CAN help.)

They are therefore forced to be self-reliant but to take advice from older people who have had similar experiences to themselves and know how to avoid the pitfalls.

A really vital point to make is that

"IT IS NOT ENOUGH TO SIMPLY WANT TO DO WELL. NOR IS IT ENOUGH TO ASSUME THAT YOU ARE GOING TO DO WELL."

Unfortunately too many millennials have been brought up to think like this. The idea that they have a right to success is one of the hurdles that you may find yourself working very hard to shift. And above all, they must not be left to think it is OK to leave it to fate.

This is where we start. The mental attitude they need to adopt is one where they believe that they can achieve their goals but only if they stick hard to a set of behaviours designed to maximize their performance.

By performance, I mean learning, understanding, passing tests of all sorts, writing good essays, doing good experiments, writing efficient notes. In fact all the things that an efficient brain should do.

They need to be good at these things. They know that they need to do this in order to pass their exams. (In a vague kind of way.) But they need to also know there is more to passing exams than the obvious study skills.

Many students find A-level study extremely hard. No news there. The new design of GCSEs which brings them much closer to the old "O" levels I taught at the start of my career, makes them seem hard, but compared to A-Levels they are not. Not because of the subject knowledge contained within them, although that is not to be sniffed at, but because the step up from GCSE to A level is like trying to vault over the Eiffel Tower. If you are an experienced teacher you will be aware of this but if you are new to the profession and have just joined the 6th form then you need to take a breath and give your charges just a tiny bit of space to allow them to acclimatise. Especially bright students who have never needed to break sweat to achieve good results.

A-level can be a rude awakening. So, this book contains advice that will help your students with this new level of difficulty.

It needs to be explained to them that in the UK, once you get into university, unless you are a complete prat, you will get your degree. The universities make sure of that by not taking on anyone they think will fail. (Unlike in some other countries.) Your degree will be hard but also fun.

So mental attitude in year 12 and 13 has to be tough. They have to be disciplined. Private schools provide this discipline. In the state sector they have to provide this for themselves.

They will probably need explaining to them exactly what this means.

Firstly, they have to go to school and they have to attend classes. This may seem obvious. In a boarding school you have no choice over this, you live on site and everyone knows where you are at more or less all times of the day. But your students may see others, in your school or college, who, once they get into the sixth form, start to think they can decide what they do and when. They will skip classes, take days off for no good reason and treat school like a drop-in centre. Their form teacher will become a distant memory!

According to Marcus Credé, Sylvia G. Roch and Urszula M. Kieszczynka (State University of New York at Albany)

> "A meta-analysis of the relationship between class attendance in college and college grades reveals that attendance has strong relationships with both class grades ($k = 69$, $N = 21,195$, $\rho = .44$) and GPA ($k = 33$, $N = 9,243$, $\rho = .41$). These relationships make class attendance a better predictor of college grades than any other known predictor of academic performance, including scores on standardized admissions tests such as the SAT, high school GPA (grade point average), study habits, and study skills."

So, **just going to classes** will get them a better grade than anything else.

As my step-father said, (Personnel Director of a large company) when I asked him what were the things he looked for in an employee.

"Get to work, get there on time, and then be a worker not a shirker."

You must make them do this.

At my school, I used to ask teachers to tell me if a student was bunking off classes, and later the SIMS system allowed me to check directly. If a student was doing this I would find them and talk to them about it. Unless there was some good reason for missing the lesson, they usually they got the message and started going to lessons. The simple fact is, you cannot learn if you are not in lessons.

Secondly they must do all tasks set, do them on time or, if possible, early.

Again, it is a matter of fact that at a private school, not doing homework is not likely to be an option.

If you do not do it, (in an ordinary state school) you will not get the benefit of having done the work. This cannot be understated.

It will also probably need explaining to them that, what is more, after a while of trying to get them to do the H/W, the teacher stops caring about them. The staff devote their attention to those who do the work and make their lives easy and gratifying. Tough, but true!

You know very well that staff hate having to chase the ones who cannot be bothered. Their mind-set is different to your students.
I am going to be just a tiny bit cynical here but it is worth running this past students as there are always at least a few staff like this in every school and they need to think about the worst case scenario.

They are employees. They may care about their students, they may not. They will do what they have to do to earn their pay and keep out of trouble. They will try and get good results, if they are nice, because they want their students to succeed. If they are not so nice, they will do it because they are judged on their results. But their lives are more complicated than their students. In a school as opposed to a sixth form college, they are mainly judged on their GCSE results, especially if they have small A-level groups. They have tons of marking and preparation and the last thing they want to do is to have a lesson prepared for a class based on a homework they have set and then to have to abandon it because too few students have done the homework.

The lesson prep has gone down the drain and they have to prepare and run a new lesson off the top of their heads. I know, I was that soldier! And I bet you have been there too.

They need to think about it and put themselves in their teachers' shoes. If they are messing up their teachers' lives why would they be positive towards such students? I always used to tell my students to come and see me at the end of the day if there was something they did not understand and they were too embarrassed to talk about in front of the class. But would I have done that if they had just bunked a lesson or not done the homework?

This is very basic but hugely important. They need to convince the staff that they care about their work. If they do that, by and large, staff will care about them. If staff do care then you will get as close as you possibly can to the small classes in private schools. The staff will go the extra mile for them, because, through their work, they are proving they are worth it. And, once they start the programme, they will become far more interested and interesting students. Staff will find themselves with students in front of them who are really on the ball and teaching will become far more enjoyable.

Thirdly, they need to be proactive in their learning. If you go over the chapters on study skills and getting the grades and really ensure they take this on board and act on it, this will put them in control of their own learning and, provided they stick with it, they will do well. This sounds harsh but in fact it is just a question of taking on new habits. Once these become second nature they will forget they ever seemed hard. And so will you. In fact you will wonder why not all teachers make them do this!

They will find themselves learning faster and feeling good about themselves. The teenage self-image being such a fragile thing this has got to be one of the best boosts they ever get and definitely leads to better grades.

Fourthly, if they have chosen the wrong A-level, they need help with making the decision whether to stick with it or not. Too many of them will try to bypass you and simply drop the difficult A-level. Try to tell them, right at the beginning that if they feel they have possibly made this sort of mistake, to come and talk to you about it. You can then both take a long, hard, cold, realistic look at the situation and decide whether he/she could pass the subject with the grade he/she needs. If they can then they should stick with it and keep telling themselves it is only for two years. (But they need to remember to be guided in their A-level choice by all the factors mentioned in the relevant chapter.) If they cannot do that, then they should drop the subject, take another one, take another year if they have to, but make sure they get the grades they need in the A-levels they need.

Lastly, they must not listen to, or be put off by, the minority of teachers who have no faith in anyone from your school doing well. Their mind-set must be, "I am going to succeed, through my own efforts, not relying on others. Others will be a help, but I have to rely on myself to get to where I want to be."

5. How to get them properly organised for study.

Getting the grades is their business. They are responsible for this. No one else. This really has to be hammered home.

Ensure that once they have got their timetable for the year, they know exactly which rooms to go to. If possible, before even going to their first lesson in a subject, this is what they should do:

Firstly, they must find out the exam board that their subject will be examined by, then go to the exam board's website and download the syllabus for the subject. <u>Then they must read it</u>!

They must do this for all their AS and A levels. (If any of your students are still doing AS levels.) This means they will have a good starting point for their studies. They will have at least a vague idea of what they will be learning about and will be able to think about where everything is leading. This is usually the first target for the small group sessions

Secondly, they must ask their teachers for copies of their schemes of work for the subjects. (Second small group target). Most teachers will give these out without batting an eyelid and may even be pleasantly surprised that students are so on the ball. Some of them may not be so forthcoming. There is no valid reason for this. You know that staff have to have these organised at all times anyway to get past OFSTED inspections, but some staff just have a bit of a hang-up about it. Tell them that if the teacher refuses to give it to them, to go and see the Head of Department or the Head of Faculty, if such a person exists, and explain that they only want these so that they can be properly prepared for lessons. I have never known this to fail. After all, what possible reason could they want this info for, other than that stated?

Once they have got these, then they really will have an idea of where they are going. Even private schools do not make their students do this.

If at all possible, they need to get their teachers to give them reading lists. They may not know what that means so they may need to have explained to them that this means lists of books that they will find useful for their subjects, to A-level and beyond.

Thirdly and most importantly, at the end of every lesson they <u>must</u> ask the teacher what they will be doing in the next lesson.

This may be completely obvious from the scheme of work, but not all teachers stick rigidly to it. Knowing what they will be doing enables them to prepare thoroughly and accurately for each lesson. (It also sharpens up the teaching - collateral effect of a positive kind!)

Fourthly, once they have this information, they must organise it into a file, one per subject at least, and then they can get on with learning in a way they have possibly never contemplated before. More in another chapter!

Fifthly, ensure that all GET A DIARY. Your school may well provide them with one, but, if not, they must get one. Then they must use it sensibly.

Many of them have no idea what this means so it is worth pointing out to them that this means more than just writing down the date a piece of work is due in. If that is all they do, then they may well find that they forget about doing it until it is too late. They must plan <u>when</u> they are going to do all the pieces of work, leaving extra time for unexpected eventualities, such as the work taking longer than they thought.

Encourage them all to put in all their social and work things, tell them they ARE allowed to have fun! And to work a bit to earn a bit of money. But do read the chapter on paid employment.

This diary must become their bible and it must be a paper document. I know it is tempting to put stuff on your phone. An iPad is better than nothing. But we all know about batteries failing at the wrong moment, chargers being left somewhere, laptops getting stolen. Who would steal a paper diary?

As a tutor you will be expecting them to bring it to all registrations and group meetings and will be expecting to see them putting targets etc., in it. Once in, it is far harder to "delete" it.

Sixthly, basic housekeeping type organisation, to ensure nothing is ever going to get in the way of their learning.

They need to be told to get transport to and from school or college organised. Organise lunch, etc. Have bags, lockers, library access, computer system access organised. Plenty of paper, files, stationery, etc., all to hand. And to not let supplies run low.

Tell them they do not want to be the idiot who turns up to class with nothing and then expects to "borrow" paper, pen, calculator, lab coat, last lesson's notes etc., from "friends". It is a cliché but failing to organise is organising to fail.

Quite simply, they want their minds clear to concentrate on the content of the lesson, which it cannot be if they are unable to make even the simplest note.

Lastly, talk to them about being in classes with friends. Try to get them to analyse their relationships with them. The reason for this is that some friends are fantastic and will really help them to learn by being in the same class as them. But others are actually a hindrance. We have all seen it. Some will just want to muck around and include your tutees in their nefarious schemes. Some will just want to use them as a shoulder to cry on because their latest boy/girlfriend has just dumped them, they had a row with their Dad, they hate their looks etc, et caetera!

Some will just want to spend as much time as possible nattering or gossiping and they will break your tutees concentration causing them to not benefit from the lesson.

They should be eased towards not sitting near these "friends".

I warned you this would be tough love, but at the end of the day, you do want them to get the best A-levels possible.

I know you may be hating me for saying this now, and that bothers me a little, because friends are important to them and no one wants to lose a friend, but get them to ask themselves, how good a friend is, if they actually get in the way of your students doing what they need to do? They can see their friends out of class and have as much fun as they like, but in class they are in business, they are at work and they need to realise that.

If they explain this to these "friends", their own grades might start to improve too.

If it is of any help to you, my tutees usually understood exactly what I was getting at and chatted to each other about friends who were "just like that". Often they just simply could not think of a friendly way of getting out of the situation. This is where the group work came in and all sorts of strategies emerged some of which were more devious than I would ever have come up with!

6. How to help them make the right A-level choice.

Why is this important? Is it too late?

A lot depends on who your student is. If he/she is a bright year 11 student then this is great, you can really give some thought to this and they can get it right, straight off the bat.

I know a lot of them will buy the companion to this eBook after having committed themselves to their A-levels. Hopefully their choices are fine, in which case you can skim through this chapter and just make sure everything is OK. Then breathe a sigh of relief and continue.

If this is not the case and they are in year 12, then things are a bit problematic, especially if you are reading this right in the middle of A-level reform.

If they are in year 13 then things are a bit tighter still and they may have to just live with their choices or else consider taking another year over A-levels in order to get themselves sorted out. (See the chapter entitled "Mind-set")

Whatever the situation, read on and make your decision accordingly. But if they want to get into a Russell Group university, or a specialised university, to do a special course, then their choice of A-level is hugely important.

Unfortunately, the best universities view the best students as being those who can handle what are often seen as the most traditional of A-levels. This does not mean that all of their A2s will have to be the hardest and most boring A-levels you can imagine, but it does mean that they need to think hard about what they are trying to do with them.

Here are some of the criteria that students have been known to use for picking their A-levels.

Fancying the teacher.

"My mate is doing it".

"It's easy".

"The teacher is fun".

"The teacher does not make you work hard".

"I get to go on trips".

"It's not boring".

Not necessarily good reasons. And this is only a short list of the most obvious ones.

Here is the list of "facilitating" subjects preferred by the Russell Group of unis.

Biology, Chemistry, Physics, Maths (and Further Maths), English Literature, History, Geography, Modern and/or Classical Languages.

And there is at least one "hot" sixth-form college in London that ONLY covers these A-levels, in fact I am not sure it even does foreign languages!

Now, this list may seem hugely boring and hard work but to the best universities these are the ones that show that a student has the ability to do well in exacting areas of study.

THESE ARE THE ONES PRIVATE SCHOOL STUDENTS DO.

GOOD NEWS. THE THREE THEY DO WILL NOT NECESSARILY HAVE TO BE THREE FROM THIS LIST.

Apart from degrees such as Medicine, usually two, max, have to be taken from this list, but they cannot take three subjects that are "(something) Studies" and hope to get into Oxford, Cambridge, Exeter, Durham, Bristol or Imperial College for example.

This is the list published by the Russell group.

Sorry! Tough love again! But vitally important. They must look long and hard at the universities they want to go to and the degree courses they think they might want to do, especially in the universities' prospectuses online. (See next chapter). They all state the A-levels they need to take. The students must take control! And not make the mistake of taking a really frivolous third A-level.

7. How to get to know your individual tutees.

This is where I ask you to put yourself in the shoes of a tutee, looking at and interacting with you.

Experienced tutors will probably have their own strategies for doing this. But even then it does no harm to have a look at some of the common problems.

"A good tutor is the person whom I should see most days. He/she should know me well, know my strengths and weaknesses and have an overall view of my needs, desires and goals."

This sounds like a mission statement. The nitty gritty of getting to really know all your tutees is not easy. Some tutees are extremely open, friendly and prepared to talk sensibly with adults of all ages. Ideal ones are not too sensitive to even the mildest of criticism or "advice". But unfortunately some are extremely hard to get to know.

This does not mean that you cannot tutor them successfully, but it often feels that you are not being successful with them.

Life is a numbers game, and in any number of tutees who pass through your hands there will inevitably be a proportion of roaring successes and a proportion of failures. All we are trying to do here is to push the number of successes up and reduce the number of failures.

It is also possible to really know a tutee well and STILL they will not achieve the success they should, so do not confuse the depth of your knowledge of a student with the chances of their success. At the end of the day, they will pass or fail on their own merits.

One thing you can do, in order to "get to know your students well", is to get them to write you a piece about themselves in which they list their achievements, their hobbies, their interests, their passions, their likes and dislikes, their ambitions. This removes them from the embarrassment of the face-to-face conversation plus it is much better to do this early on so that things can be rectified in plenty of time before they are preparing for UCAS, e.g. if they really need to do something about any lack of interesting features to put into the personal statement.

Sometimes what you discover is amazing, some of them will be carers, some of them will have outstanding achievements. I once had a boy who was the 10th best dancer in the world in some form of modern dance, he never talked about it until after he had written this down.

It is also good to realise your tutees limits. Sometimes this is due to massive lack of confidence. One of my students made mens' clothes. She was outstanding and should have gone straight to one of the big fashion design schools. She did consider for a while going to Paris to study and spent a lot of time in fashion houses in London on work placements, but in the end she did not feel confident enough to leap right in, so she ended up on an arts foundation course. But I am sure she will get there in the end and she has promised to make me a suit once she has got there!

Another girl was a real beauty with a 38 inch inside leg measurement. It was obvious to all who knew her that she should have gone into modelling. But she lacked confidence, was extremely shy and quite simply did not want to do it. Much as my granddaughter who was three times offered a place at the Royal Ballet School. She kept turning them down as she, also, simply did not want to do it.

What I am trying to say here is that we cannot make their decisions for them, we cannot live their lives for them, we must understand their desires and go along with them while at the same time ensuring that they give themselves the best possible chance of maximising their success in their chosen field.

Of course the opposite end of the scale is a problem too. The student who wants to be a cardiac surgeon but is really not very good at science. Or the would-be fighter pilot who is too tall and scatter-brained. These are usually easier to deal with.

It eventually dawns on them as time goes on and they simply do not get the grades. Or they join the ATC and find difficulty in landing a glider.

You just have to let them down gently, commiserate and help them find something they are more suited to.

We need to get in touch with our tutees but not try to be their friend. It is a fine line to draw, but an objective viewpoint is essential if we are to serve our students the best we can.

I have come across the odd tutor who spent far too much time trying to be matey with his/her tutees. It was tooth-curling to witness and the tutees hated them but couldn't show it. Rather like the parent who tells you, "I am my child's best friend."

Mentally I was screaming at them, "Then who in heaven's name is their parent? Who sets the boundaries?"

On another tack, sometimes you will be in a situation where it is vital that you see the student on his/her own. This tends to occur when the position is such that he/she does not want to have witnesses to the necessary conversation, i.e. the sub-group situation is not right for it.

Do not jump right in and have the meeting when the tutee is not expecting it. Tell the student you want to see him/her, tell them what it will be about and tell them when you want to see them. It may well be best to send them an email or write them a note rather than smash the whole point of the exercise by saying it in front of others. And if you ask them to just "Stay behind for a minute" the others will all know something is up and put them in a position they may not want to be in.

The last thing they will need is other tutees grilling them about "What's that about then?"

If you do not feel confident about seeing them on their own, or they don't, give them the option of bringing a friend along, but be aware that this can be a double-edged sword. If the friend starts to try and get involved in the conversation in a way in which this will become unproductive, then be prepared to call a halt to it and move to the next stage.

Then think about where the meeting will be, can it be in a private setting, a semi-public place, or would you rather have a member of year staff with you?

If things are at that stage it may well be better to hand the job on, at least to an extent, to another member of Year staff, but try to nip all problems in the bud.

The bond between you both will not be improved if the student feels you cannot talk to him/her or worse, they cannot talk to you. And after any conversation with more senior staff, they will still have to come back to working with you.

It never happened to me but I have heard of tutees being moved out of tutor groups due to some lack of empathy between them and their tutor. Indeed, I sometimes found myself with extra students at the beginning of a term due to this happening in another tutor group. You may well find this happening to you, especially if you are a good tutor.

Be aware that it is not a reason to celebrate! Some of them can be very difficult to get to know. I am reminded of one particularly arrogant student who felt he knew everything and that he needed no help. He was determined to get onto a particular degree course of which there is only one in the country. He eventually did, but only after an extra year and then being offered a place because someone else did not turn up!

You should know what they are doing in their "frees", you should influence them into good use of this time and good use of all school resources. You should also be aware of all outside activities that have a bearing on their wellbeing, their ability to learn to the max and anything else that can be useful to them in the furtherance of their career and university application.

There is advice about all this in other chapters, but you should know enough about them, without prying into their private life, to ensure that nothing is getting in the way of their chances of success.

I apologise to all experienced tutors for whom this is all old hat. I am not being patronising, I am just writing for tutors at all stages of their careers.

At the end of the day, if the tutee is working well and going to get the grades, then the only other thing you really need to worry about, provided they are happy, or reasonably so, is the reference and the personal statement on the UCAS form.

This is why you need in depth knowledge of them, to inform your helping them with the personal statement and the part of the reference which is your responsibility.

8. How to ensure their Study Skills are REALLY effective.

By the end of GCSE, especially if they obtained good grades, they may think they are pretty well skilled-up and do not need much help. But they are almost on their own now.

GCSEs are (or were pre 2015) sooo easy compared to AS and A-levels.

In order to do well at the higher level, their study skills need to be stratospheric, quite apart from the fact that once they have acquired a new way of studying independently, their university life will be so easy compared to their peers who will not have benefited from this way of thinking. And again, not even private schools give their students this.

Spoon-feeding is out from now on. By this I mean that, at GCSE, many if not all of their teachers will probably have given them all the learning they needed in bite-sized chunks. All they needed to do was to regurgitate it in the exam and they would get a good grade. Nothing was too difficult. They would have practised all the tests with their teachers, who would have practically written their coursework for them, (if they had any), they would hardly have had to make any notes as everything would have been given to them in hand-outs. You may feel I am exaggerating but I have personal knowledge of teachers who taught like this.

Some A-levels are a bit like that and all they need to do is to have a good memory. But in many cases, they have to be able to analyse, to write a good essay, to understand complicated theories, etc. If they go to lessons not knowing what is going to come their way, and they sit down, open that lid on the top of their heads and wait for the teacher to pour the knowledge into their brains, they may find themselves in trouble. Stuff may go past them and by the time they realise they did not get it, the teacher may well have moved on.

They look around, their mates didn't get it either and simply shrug and shake their heads. Then the cold, clammy clutch of fear goes around their hearts and they realise that they do not get what is going on. They panic, quietly, inwardly. They think they are stupid. They think they have taken the wrong A-level. They blame the teacher for going too fast.

All this can happen and I have known of students in tears, students who drop out of an A-level etc, all because of this sort of thing happening to them.

Often this was an over-reaction but almost all students have moments like this whether on a similar scale or at a lower level.

Some students need to have it explained to them that they realistically have to switch their own brains on and make efforts to understand difficult concepts rather than simply expecting to understand complicated ideas just by being in the same room as the teacher.

So, what can they do to avoid the "clammy clutch of fear"? The answer is not as complicated as they may think. They already have both the syllabus and the scheme of work. Before all lessons, they must read up on the content of the lesson to come, so that when they go in, they know what to expect. They have already had time to ponder on any difficulties they may encounter; in fact they are properly prepared for the lesson. Again, private schools do not make their students do this.

Resources for this are not hard to find. You and your colleagues will be aware of them, and you can tell your students that the internet is usually a good start for studies below degree level, there will be books in the school, college or local library or they may have a course-book. Encourage them to go mad and BUY some books! Get them second-hand from Amazon! Their parents or grandparents may even be persuaded to buy them for them. They do not cost much more than a half-decent burger!

The buzz they will get from doing this will be really obvious the first time they go to a lesson so well prepared.

It also means that they will know exactly what questions they need to ask the teacher for clarification.

Let them know that teaching yourself is more efficient than being taught, without boring them with the psychology of it all. They must be in a position to treat the teacher as simply a great learning and verifying resource.

What if they have tried reading up on something and they still do not get it? This is where the questions that they ask the teacher come into their own. This is what lessons should be used for.

Does your school or college have peer mentors? And I do not mean groups of students prepared to sit around with each other drinking coffee while they pour their heart out about how they are not getting on with their parents, boy/girlfriend, peers, weight problem, etc.

I mean study groups. There is too much about these to mention here so I have devoted a separate chapter to this subject.

The third thing that they should do, which again private school students will not necessarily be told to do, (apologies to any private school teacher reading this who does his/her job properly, but what are you doing reading this book, may I ask!?) is to read around the subject.

This needs explaining to them. That it means getting books out or using the internet to find out as much as they can about the subject. They may need taking to the library and showing how to use indexes and the Dewey Decimal system. Show them that not only will this give them different perspectives, and/or different ways of understanding, but it will also provide them with insights into parts of the subject they had not been told about or had not thought about.

If they really like their subjects, and at A-level they really should, then this should be fun. Even if this isn't the case, it at least may provide them with quotes and/or topics they can use at university interviews or in their personal statements.

Apart from this, there are individual study skills that they will need to acquire to go with the specific subjects they are taking. This can vary from "how to dissect a rat" to "how to use the imperfect subjunctive". These skills are too specific to be fitted into a small volume like this, but if they have taken on board the ideas presented to them so far, they will understand that they need to find resources to help them, be it paper, internet, video, You Tube (God help education!), or another person! They just need to be sure that the person they are talking to does know their facts and are preferably properly qualified or at least on their course.

These study skills they will find a godsend once they get to university, especially as they will find out so quickly that the internet is useless for degree level studies. What the people around them will be finding hard, they will be doing easily, without having to think about it. I know this is true as ex-students of mine have stayed in touch and have told me how much they appreciated already having these vital skills. In fact some of them went straight on to become subject representatives in their subjects in the first year of their degrees, which I felt very chuffed about.

9. What Study Groups are and how your tutees can use them to their advantage.

Depending on your school or college, you may already be aware of these.

What I found when I was at school was that when a teacher went too fast, or explained something badly, I had only a few choices to try and help me understand what I was supposed to have got from the lesson. I found one of the best things was to go and speak to a friend doing the same course who had a better grasp of what was going on. In essence, this is what a study group is.

Your students may be doing exactly what I did, but can they be sure that the person they are talking to really does have a handle on the subject? Or is it just a case of the partially-sighted leading the blind?

In order to ensure that their understanding of a subject is more complete, and also to help motivate themselves when things are not going as well as they would wish, it may well be a good idea to help them join a study group or start one. If your school is switched on, it will already have these and certain students will be designated as subject mentors. If this is not the case then might I suggest you mention it to your Head of 6th? It is not hard to find students who are on top of their game in a certain subject and to get them to make themselves available on a regular or ad hoc basis to help lead study groups.

They are also great when it comes to revision time. If your Head of Sixth is useless, or does not like the idea because he/she did not think of it first, then I suggest you get your tutees to rally round and organise things informally. And by that I mean with other students outside the tutor group as well. They do not have to take place on the school premises. Although it would take an amazingly obtuse member of the Senior staff of your school to not see the benefit of these groups, and to thus set rooms aside where possible for you to use.

In my last job we had about 30 study groups running, about half of which were led by members of my tutor group. If any of your students find themselves running one of these groups there is no doubt that it will deepen their understanding of your subject. As a teacher you will be all too aware that there is nothing like explaining something to someone else, to make you really concentrate on getting it 100% right. (It also looks good when mentioned in a UCAS personal statement.) So whether they use them to learn or to advance the learning of others, they will definitely benefit.

10. How to make sure they get the necessary grades.

This is a long chapter hence the subtitles.

What is meant by "necessary grades".

The learning process.

The five step approach.

What is meant by "necessary grades".

At this point you are probably saying, "Hang on this is impossible. I cannot do this, even their teachers cannot do this, what is he on about?"

Please bear with me. Perhaps I should have re-entitled it, "...make sure they get the best possible..." But that is wishy-washy and I do not think like that.

First of all, if you have done your best and your students have too, to ensure they have chosen courses at university for which they CAN gain the entrance grades, i.e. that they have been realistic about, then that is the "necessary grades".

Ensure they understand that, without wishing to state the obvious, if they do not get the grades, they do not get the places.

It may need explaining that it may say in the prospectus that for a certain course you only need BCB, or a certain point count, to get on the course they are looking at, but they cannot rely on that. It depends on whether the course tutor is a "chooser" or a "filler".

If the course is oversubscribed, if out of 100 candidates, 98 get BBB or above, then if there are only 30 places, they cannot bitch if they do not get a place, even with BCB.

So, their first goal is to get AT LEAST the grades required in the university's prospectus and/or by the offer.

If they have left it to this point to work for good grades, they have left it somewhat late. But never say die. Realistically, they need to get the best possible grades they can, and as far above what the university says it is looking for, as possible.

All subjects vary, although some, e.g. languages or sciences, have similarities, but explain to them that their strategies for getting the correct grade in each subject are not that different.

As with much of what this book covers, organisation is the key.

The Learning process.

They need to understand thoroughly the learning process in order to ensure that they are taking the correct steps to maximise their grades. (I apologise in advance if you know all this stuff, maybe you do, maybe you don't, but bear in mind I am writing this for all sorts of tutors.)

This is one of the longest and most detailed chapters in the book, I hope it is useful to you!

Learning involves acquiring skills and knowledge, but passing exams involves more than just having the facts and figures in your memory. During the exam period they need to be able to demonstrate, in a very artificial way, that they possess certain knowledge, and can prove this via arguing a case, or doing exercises, as in Maths or other science subjects.

They may have to prove this through a practical test, or a long piece or research and coursework, or simply by answering questions on the paper.

Whatever form of test the exam takes, they will have to have acquired the necessary skills and knowledge to prove to the examiners that they are worthy of the grade.

So we are going to break the exam preparation business down into smaller, bite-sized chunks, so that they realise it is all possible and there is no real reason why they should not get a top grade in all their subjects.

They should use the syllabus to break the subject down into each of the individual areas that they will be covering.

The five step approach.

For each area they will need:

To understand it
To know it
To be able to recall it
To practise it
To be able to prove their knowledge, (the exam.)

It is hugely important that they realise that although linked, each of these five things is distinct.

Understanding it.

One normally cannot "know" something without understanding it.

The "understanding" part of the subject area is the part the teacher is supposed to help you with. This is bit of a statement. Of course, the teacher ought to be helping with ALL of them, but, life being what it is, this may not happen. But he/she must try to help with understanding.

So, what should they do if they are having problems understanding a topic?

First off, get the teacher to explain the concept in as many ways as she/he can. If that does not work, read it up, if that doesn't work, go through it with the study group. Use the internet and the library. If all else fails, be prepared to have to learn it off by heart. But this is usually not necessary.

If this happens to one of them, they may feel a bit of a failure. They MUST NOT. Many students, even very bright ones, find there are parts of a syllabus they simply have to learn off by heart. The only proviso is that they must still be able to answer any question on this topic in an exam. If they answer it successfully, it does not matter whether they fully understood it or not, as long as they can prove they know it!

There are parts of most syllabi that this applies to, so tell them not to sweat it. To just be aware that they may have to do this. (See "Revision, exam prep and past papers")

Knowing it.

This you might think of as "learning".

Some of the time it may well be this. Some A-level subjects are long on facts and short on understanding concepts. Many students do very well at A-level because they have very good memories. But there are many ways of "learning" things.

Books have been written on "memory". Psychologists, brainiacs of all types, have tried to study how we learn, and they have made some headway, (ouch, sorry for the pun), but no one really knows a sure-fire way of ensuring total recall. But it helps if they understand a bit about how memory works. (Once again apologies...etc)

The following is one way of explaining things that I have found works for me. If it doesn't work for you then no problem, use whatever works for you, but it IS important that they have some idea of how memory works in order to be able to make best use of theirs.

Explain to them that, first off, remembering a fact is about _two_ things, putting in into your memory and then getting it back out again.

Your brain is a complicated son-of-a-gun, and it does all sorts of things to try and help you in your life. One thing it does is to kind of filter the stuff you are doing all the time, to sort it into "important" and "unimportant". This is what is shown up when a witness in a court case is asked the question, "Do you remember what the defendant was wearing when you saw him last?" If you are like me, you'd be pushed to remember in any detail, because my brain would have filed the clothes under "unimportant".

We all forget stuff and we all know how infuriating it can be, but we all know it happens. Why is this? Well broadly, we tend to remember things according to their level of importance. And how often we use them. The most important we remember without making any effort whatsoever. Like how to walk. How to swallow. How to interpret what we see. We do not even notice we are doing these things. But things like remembering your mum's or dad's birthday? Whoops! Suddenly the importance is obvious, but sadly sometimes your brain "let's you down" and you say "It just slipped my memory".

Some psych people are convinced that ALL the detail of everything we have ever seen is in our heads somewhere, like a perpetually running CCTV camera, but the problem is RECALLING it.

Being able to recall it.

Point out to them that if you decide, consciously, that you want to remember something, it is not enough to simply say to your brain, "Hey there, remember this thing". If it were, there would be no problem. But again, the brain "comes to the rescue" by deciding to forget things for you! So you have to overpower this. Understanding why this happens may help.

And you only need to remember something until after you have passed the exam! If you need it again, a little bit of work will bring it back. There are theories about "forgetting", one being that without this system, your brain would just get so crowded it could not function. Imagine if you could not forget. You would have last week's shopping list overlaying the shape of the cloud you just looked at overlaying the smell of the dog this morning overlaying ljily fou jyg kljp igkni.   You get the message. You would go mental.

So we must forget what is unimportant and remember what is not. So we have to take charge.

Tell them that when you first put something in your memory, it goes into "short term" memory. This is a place you can recall it from for a while but then disappears, or at least appears to.

Here's a bit of fun you could have with your group to prove it to them. Read out a series of numbers, make them wait a few seconds, and then make them write them down. Each time make the number a digit longer. (Start with 4). By the end you will have established a couple of things.

Firstly that short term memory has a finite capacity. For numbers it varies between about 7 and 10 digits.

Secondly, ask all the students to turn their pieces of paper over at the end of the test, then ask them to write down the 3rd number you gave them. This proves to them that short term memory has finite time limits. Most of them will not remember it, although it was written there on the other side of the piece of paper, only a few minutes ago.

So how do you remember/recall stuff?

First it has to be transferred to "long term" memory. Secondly methods have to be devised to recall it from this. This frankly is done via repetition and variety.

Remembering, or recall, involves neural pathways. These are the links between the memory, which is buried in a brain cell somewhere, (long term memory) and the outside world, i.e. your ability to say it, do it, picture it etc.

http://www.ldonline.org/article/5602/

explains this, although it seems to apply to young children the premises are still correct for all learning.

Tell them to imagine they have been given a small, gold ingot and are told to put it in a little box and go and place it on the grass in the middle of a field. They then have to leave it there and walk to the gate. The following day they are told they have 5 minutes to find it. They stand at the gate and, with any luck, can see it. They go straight to it and pick it up. Then they are told to replace it and walk out of the field. They then have to go back a week later. They stand at the gate but the grass has grown, they cannot see it. They spend at least part of the 5 minutes frantically walking around the area where they think they left it. They may find it, they may not. This is the equivalent of having lost the neural pathway to the item in long-term memory.

The ingot is still there, they know it is still there, they just cannot find it. But if they find it, they are given another 10 minutes to do something to make sure they can find it again. Think how many different things they could do to make sure they never lost the precious gold ingot? If they are scientific, they could use a compass to take a bearing from the gate and then count the number of paces they need to walk. Or they could use the compass to triangulate the position of the box on three different features around the field, or they could simply spend the ten minutes walking back and forth from the gate to the box, trampling the grass as they go.

This is the equivalent of building in a solid recall mechanism or neural pathway as it is called. And obviously it works.

Then they are allowed to go back to the field but only in the middle of a very dark moonless night. The compass is no use; can they feel the trampled grass? Maybe. Can they smell it? Maybe. What about the person who used a piece of string and two pegs. He/she would have no problem.

This is metaphorical recall. Trying to find something hidden in a field of grass, is like trying to recall a piece of information, "hidden" in your memory. You know it's there, but can you get to it?

This is what happens if you do not do practice papers. If you knew you would have to be able to find it in the dark, this would be the equivalent of knowing the type of question you would get in the exam, and you would prepare more thoroughly for it.

Recall from long term memory means having to reuse the information in a MEANINGFUL way quite a few times, before it sinks in and can be easily recalled. This is straight-forward repetition. The more it is used, the more you will remember it. But it may not be something easily used. So you need to think of a variety of different ways of remembering it. Or more accurately, recalling it.

This is because the more, different neural pathways you can use to recall a piece of information, the better your chances of recalling it. This is like having three or four different ways of finding your box.

There are places on the internet where you can discover your best individual learning style or styles suited to you personally. (Google "Discover your learning style").

We are all different and this is a big help. You should strongly advise them do this and then put this knowledge into action to improve their revision and recall.

Here are some sorts of things people use to help recall.

Mnemonics, for example. Love them or hate them, they work for a lot of people. You may need to explain what they are: simple memory aids that help recall more complex ideas or pieces of information. I can still remember a mnemonic I was taught, the pre-flight checklist for a glider. I went on a one week gliding course with the ATC and that was 45 years ago, but I can still remember it.

Other people have their own ways of developing recall.

They write their notes out over and over again, (rather onerous).

They make shorter, condensed notes (good one).

They repeat bits out loud, thus using three neural pathways instead of just one, (they have to (one) read it, (two) say it and they will (three) hear themselves say it. Three times as efficient as just reading it.

They test themselves.

They visualize the steps or the material or provide themselves with visual cues.

They get their friends to test them.

They have packs of cards with notes written on them and use them for various games.

They make up raps, or songs or poems.

They draw diagrams over and over again.

"Mind maps", some people love them.

They could make up PowerPoint presentations, if they have the time.

Some things work better than others for everybody. But nothing works better than having to explain something to someone else. (As a teacher you know this better than almost anyone.)

Or having to DO something with the thing you are trying to remember. So teaching someone else about something helps you master it.

Every time you use another part of your body to practise a piece of knowledge, then your brain needs to use a totally different neural pathway to find the brain cell with the knowledge in it. This is where repetitively writing notes out can help. But it is very time consuming and not something I would recommend, purely on that basis.

But ask any musician, he/she will tell you that the only way to be able to play a really fast passage is to practise it until they get it "under their fingers". On concert night, the adrenalin may have speeded up the brain to the point where they can actually play it from the music, but it cannot be guaranteed. The same is true of touch typing. You may not realise it, but if you type often enough on a keyboard, you may in fact have accidentally learned where the letters are. Get them to try it out. Simply shut your eyes. Then try and type something. You may be surprised at how much you get right. Your brain has learned the positions of the keys without you realising, through constant repetition.

Writing notes out or writing the answer to an essay question uses more than just memory skills, it involves organising your ideas and then writing them down. Thus multiplying the neural pathways.

Being forced to do this helps recall skills.

They need, as individuals, to find methods or varieties of methods that work for them. But they must be aware that mindlessly staring at a book, or their notes, even if they read them 20 times over, is no substitute for actually using the knowledge.

Practising it.

We've already touched on some of this, but they must bear in mind that remembering stuff to themselves or to a friend is not the same as doing it in an exam room under pressure. Practice has to be made the same as an exam without all the pressure. (The exam pressure comes from having limited time to do the business in, as well as having no access to any notes or books.) The only way to do this is to answer practice exam questions. You and your colleagues should be giving them these, they should take them in and then "mark" them. Having done this for nearly 34 years I can tell you what happened. Some students did the work, looking up what they needed to look up, (if it was allowed, some still did it anyway), trying their best to answer the question(s) fully and accurately, then they handed it in. They then took it back, read all my remarks and did their best to learn from their mistakes. Others did not do this! (You do not need to guess which ones did the best in their exams.) They often could not be bothered to really use it as practice. They didn't do it, or they didn't take it seriously. Or they cheated, by looking stuff up, or doing it as a group effort with their mates. Then they may not have handed it in on time.

At this point you can then explain that the teacher may well get fed up with this (I certainly did) and only give it a cursory look-over, a mark and maybe a one sentence comment. "You gets what you pays for" (this was never a comment! Just a reflection of what you get back if you do not put in the effort).

If they do it properly the teacher will probably take it seriously and give them good feedback. They should not just look at the mark and then ask their mates what they got! They should READ the remarks and pay attention to them. You know as well as I do that many A-level teachers have been A-level exam markers and really know what they are doing. Whatever they write, they must pay it the respect it deserves and take it all in. Even if it seems negative.

If the teacher is not doing this, then they should ask them what they need to do to improve their work, especially if the mark was not as good as they expected. I know that Ofsted is jumping all over this and that it is much less likely they will have non-comment-making staff, but you never know!

They must be aware that exam boards publish Past Papers and mark schemes for them. The more often an exam format is changed, the fewer Past Papers of the right type there will be. But it needs explaining to them that, although it is not ideal, doing older style Past Papers will do them no harm because, after all, the subject has not changed that much, if at all, and the practice will still do them good.

(There is much more to Past Paper use in a later chapter.) They MUST do past papers before their exams. (Mind boggling to imagine a teacher not doing this, but it does happen, especially if the teacher for some reason is struggling to finish the syllabus before the exam.

Some of my tutees had experience of this.)

Marking their own work.

Again, nowadays this is seen as normal practice, by most schools, but I have to imagine that there are still schools where this is not happening. If your school is like this then welcome to the 21st century! By the time they sit down to do their mock exams, and especially their real ones, they should have such an accurate idea of their own performance that they can go through the paper they have just answered and give themselves marks. They should get used to mentally marking their own work right from day one of the course. Before handing it in. This will give them real self-knowledge.

Comparing what they thought they should have got to what they actually got, gives them a really good idea of where they are accurate about their own abilities and knowledge. This will help focus their revision.

We have all come across the sight and sound of a student handing in a piece of work and saying "I have no idea how well I did in that". That student is not looking at what the question required, has no idea of how to answer the question and has no idea of how much of the answer was accurate or relevant. "Clueless" is the only word for them.

That sort of attitude will not get anyone a good grade. Don't let this be your students. I did this for my degree exams and I was never more than 5% out. This self-knowledge is vital. I trained my tutees to do this and some of them got 100% in exams and in one case the student actually knew it before he saw the grade. Easier maybe because it was Maths, but still, he got to Imperial College London.

So they must do this all the time, and if they realise they have missed something or not fully understood something, it should be obvious before they get the marked work back. This then gives them a starting point for revision. (See relevant chapter).

https://www.opencolleges.edu.au/informed/learning-strategies/10-ways-to-retain-more-of-what-you-learn/

This site explains what I have just written, if you want a different way of looking at it.

Proving it, (Exam technique.)

Having all the knowledge in the world at your fingertips is worth nothing if you cannot get it down on paper for the examiners.

This is where exam technique comes in. They are in a race against the clock to understand the questions, see what the examiner is getting at and what they have to be able to explain or relate, and then to write it all down clearly and succinctly in the time allowed.

If they are of a nervous disposition, they may find that their nerves make this whole thing even more difficult. We have all heard of the student who just goes into a blue funk, stares at the paper, and then makes a total hash of it, or runs screaming out of the exam hall. This is why, at exam times, some universities have to take special precautions with high buildings, to try to ensure students do not panic and jump off them.

I DO understand the pressure that some of them feel they are under. I am sure you do too. If this really is a medical condition, then for heaven's sake get them to a doctor and get them to write a medical note for them, which will be taken into consideration by the exam board.

Try to make it clear to them that this is not a sign of weakness, it is just the way some people are and is a natural thing. More importantly, he/she may well give them medication and other techniques to try to help them overcome their nerves.

But if they are just common-or-garden nervous, then here are a few things they can try, and I am sure you have your own personal ideas on the topic.

Practise breathing techniques. They'll probably find them all over the internet.

Ensure they get organised before the exam and get into a routine. I always used to wear my "lucky jacket". Mainly because it had enough pockets to be able to put all my stuff in.

They need to have a routine so that they do not waste time looking for stuff, or panicking about it.

They must check at least three times that they have everything they need and the time of the exam. (Have you heard of staff rushing off to a student's home to pick them up and take them to the exam they got the time wrong for? I have!)

They should have routines before the exams - eating, transport, who they talk to and who they stay away from! That sort of thing. (This helps with the nerves.)

Once in the exam room, try to get them to not think about the importance of the exam. They do not need to. They KNOW it is important. They must not think about big stuff like success or failure. They should remember that whatever they have done to prepare themselves for the exam is now done.

They must only think 5 minutes ahead, to the next thing they must do. They must look forward.

Tell them that, as soon as they can open the paper, they should do so, to go through it thoroughly but quickly. There should not be any surprises and they may find themselves inwardly leaping for joy when they read a question or two that they just know they can do in their sleep. (But they must guard against overconfidence)

They must remember exam boards are not allowed to set EXACTLY the same questions as they have in past papers. This is actually extremely hard, (I know, I have had to do this!) But the questions will be asking for the same knowledge and the same techniques to be used. (This is like knowing you will be going into the field containing the gold ingot in daylight.)

They must make sure they read the question until they understand exactly what the examiner is getting at.

If they have a choice of questions, they must take extra care to choose the correct ones for them.

They must make sure they answer enough questions, and not too many. I have known of cases where a student has mistakenly tried to answer all the questions on a paper!

They absolutely must READ the RUBRIC! It has been known for an exam board to change the format of an exam slightly.

They must not fall in to the trap of selling themselves short by not answering sufficient questions.

They need to be told to "set their stalls out". Using the clock or their watches (if allowed) to work out how much time, roughly, they can devote to each question. Explain they do not have to stick to this rigidly but to use it as a guide as to when to move on. (If they have done enough past papers this should be second nature.) And let them know they should try to leave time for checking.

If the worst comes to the worst, they can use this to finish, if they have over-run a bit but they must try not to be in this situation.

Ensure they understand that when answering the question, they should keep reminding themselves what the question is and stick to ONLY answering it. Once they have done that, to move on. They must not feel tempted to show off on a question about a topic they love. They are only wasting their own time. They cannot gain more marks than the question is worth.

Tell them NOT TO WAFFLE. If they cannot answer the question, they must live with it and spend the time answering the other questions as well as they can. Warn them that if they know they are going to run out of time, they must not just plough on regardless. They must start just writing bullet points with the key points in them. The examiner will at least then know that they have some idea of the answer. They may not get full marks but at least they should be credited with some of them.

But they must try like mad not to get into this position.

If they have stuck to their timing and have time to go through the work, they should use this critically to ensure they have not made basic errors, like misunderstanding the question or making simple arithmetical errors. Or have left something out.

If they have enough time, they should mentally mark the work and work out what grade they should get! I actually used to enjoy doing that, and I did get the grade of degree I thought I should get.

Explain to them that they must not be surprised if they enjoy doing exams. That is quite normal. They should be able to enjoy proving themselves. I used to pride myself on getting every candidate to laugh at least once during their oral exam. It helped the candidate to relax and many of them actually said they enjoyed the exam, to their surprise and it did not hurt their grades one bit.

Above all, tell them to ensure the practical bits are done, their name and number is wherever it needs to be, pages are all linked together, etc. Bits of my daughter's Physics A-level paper went missing. No one would admit to it, she was given a U. Even after a re-mark. At retake she got a B and this was in the late nineties. I don't think it was her fault but tell your charges not to let that happen to them.

After the exam.

Once out of the exam room, advise them against going and chatting with the sort of mates who want to do a "post mortem" on the exam. It does not help in the slightest. It tends to be depressing. Tell them "It's over, move on, look forward to the next one you will be doing, the next bit of revision you'll be doing or simply getting some R and R."

To sum up, understand, learn, recall, practice, exam technique. These are the keys to getting the grades.

11. Showing them how to maximise effective use of study periods.

They may, (probably will) simply call these "frees". And if they do, this actually says a lot about them.

If they look on these as free time, then they need to rethink their approach. But you know this already, here is how to ensure they realise how effective use of this time can simplify their lives and ensure good grades, as well as increase the enjoyment of their subjects.

To start with the basics, where can, or do, they work?

The answer tends to depend, at least to a certain extent, on the subjects they are studying. Practical subjects necessitate use of school or college equipment, and they may well have to use their study periods to use this stuff.

But if not, there should be a library or resource centre they can use, or even special rooms set aside. This will depend on the establishment. Some simply do not have the space to accommodate all the students, this was certainly the problem in the school I worked in.

Or, there may be space but the other students may make so much noise that they cannot concentrate. Or they may not like using noise-cancelling headphones.

If they live a short distance from home, and getting to and from your school/college is not an issue, then it may be better for them to work there, when appropriate. But this means they have to be shown how to ensure they work when they get home.

Many students do have that self-discipline, but you don't need me to tell you that they may well find themselves doing things that are non-productive. My advice, if this is a possibility for them, is to encourage them to develop a routine that ensures they make full use of the time. Telling their parent(s) or whoever might be at home once they get there, what interruptions they are happy with. Mum bringing them a cup of tea may well be fine, but mum barging in to chat with them, or worse still row with them, certainly is not. They need to think seriously about this and get a clear understanding with their responsible adult. Also they have to be people who work best on their own, and this means without the distractions of computer (not being used constructively), iPhone, iPad, television or whatever. "Get in, switch the phone off and get on" has to be their motto. But trusting them to work at home is a sign of them growing up and if they can prove to you that this is successful then a mild indication of respect for their step into adulthood will be a positive move.

In any case, they need a workspace organised so that they can work properly in the evenings and weekends. I, and you, will appreciate that not all young people have their own rooms, and that this makes things difficult. If this is their circumstance, then they need to think creatively, is there somewhere else they could set up a table and a light? A room that is not much used, (the dining room for me when I was young)? A shed? A garage? Granny's place? A Public library? A friend's house? Where there is a will, there is a way.

Once they have a work space, and this is going to sound really drastic, they should consider putting a weekly planner on the OUTSIDE of the door. Why the outside? Well, if their self-discipline falters, and they get on well enough with their parent(s), then they could enlist their help to give them gentle reminders and to ensure they keep on top of assignments and other planned tasks. This has worked for many of my tutees. But if the last thing they want is one or both parents breathing down their necks, then they should not bother. (They should then put the planner up inside the room somewhere.) Obviously this should tie in with their diary.

So what IS the best use of these times?

Do they plan them along with the rest of the time they can control? Do they just use them for doing homework or other assignments?

They <u>must plan</u> their study periods. If they don't, then the time just flies by, no matter how good their intentions are.

Cups of coffee in the common room, or whatever your place calls it, "before I start", often take up half a "free". Why not force themselves to use official break times only and to resist the urge to take more breaks than that? Their consciences will be far happier every time they complete a task.

So, what do they plan to do? The obvious things to be getting on with are written assignments, practical assignments and **reading around the subject.** The last thing in this group is something that some students never do. They have no idea what it is; no one ever says they should be doing it so they don't do it. They may well do all their homework, hand it in on time, go to all lessons and even get good grades, but if they do, they are lucky. If they then get into the university of their choice then it may well be because they already go to an enlightened school/college where the staff give them assignments which are basically reading lists, or other tasks which force them to do reading in order to achieve.

Bear in mind that in the chapter about getting properly organised, I mentioned the need to read up on the subjects in the syllabus and the schemes of work before each lesson. This is something they should regard as a necessity, not just a luxury. Reading around the subject brings it to life, makes it enjoyable, more practical maybe, and certainly gives them food for thought, and avenues leading to further thinking about the subject.

If they cannot think where to start, which books to read, they should ask their teacher to recommend something. For example, I taught French A-level, and I used to lend students easy literature books, not at all linked to the syllabus, but fun to read and something that gave them a real sense of using the language and something to discuss either with me or with friends doing the same A-level, or, obviously, at university interview. They gave insights into philosophy, culture etc.

Imagine if the interviewer asks them what books they have read on their subject and they are forced to answer, "Well, none, actually, it wasn't part of the syllabus."

This is a hugely important part of their education, they are probably doing only 3 subjects (possibly 4) they DO have "free time" their school days are short, in comparison with 17/18 year olds elsewhere in the world so they cannot say, "Oh I can't do that, I don't have the time/energy for it." They certainly do and it must not be forgotten that they are up against all the other private school people who will probably be doing this type of reading.

If they doubt this time issue, try the following exercise with them. Get them to actually add up the time they spend per week doing everything, and then take that away from the 216 hours in a week. Having done this regularly with my tutor groups I can tell you they are amazed by the amount of time that ends up being unaccounted for. Where does this time go?

Once they sit and think about it, they will find that at least some of it can be profitably used for their education.

Study periods can also be profitably used for discussions with study groups. These they must come to see as friends who WILL help them with their work rather than those who WON'T, i.e. the ones who want them to chat with them about anything other than work, beg them to go and have a coffee with them, or to kick a football about.

The most important point to be taken from this chapter is that "study periods" should be exactly that, and if they do not use them properly then they are short-changing themselves. They must make sure they plan everything, put it in their diary and stick to it.

At one of your sessions with them, early in the first term you will find it useful to get them to write out a plan for a fortnight as to how they will use their study periods. This to be put in the diary. Tell them that at the next session they will be required to show it to you with details as to what exactly they did in these times. This will crystallise their minds and get them to plan and record this time as well as all other working times. If any of them seem to be recalcitrant about this, let them know that you will be looking at this every time you see them, until you are satisfied that they really are using this time properly. This usually is not necessary, as most of them will see the sense of it from the off, but just in case...

12. Showing them how to make best use of genuine free time.

You may well wonder what on earth this is going to be about. Don't worry; I am not going to tell you to preach at them about what they should be doing when not studying or working. All I am going to do is suggest you ask them to think just a tiny little bit about what they can do during the free time they have, which could be enjoyable and yet increase their chances of getting that university place they want.

What??????????????!!!!!!!!!!!

Ok, here we go.

As I said in the chapter on what private schools do that ordinary schools don't, I explained how students there live much more regimented lives. But they also have marvellous opportunities to indulge in pastimes, sport, hobbies etc., all of which, if your students did some of them, would make them look more interesting on their UCAS personal statement.

Just to give you some idea, at my Public school, I played tennis, squash, rugby (for the school), cricket, did rowing and athletics and I became a corporal in the ATC. I also learned to play the piano, the guitar and the trumpet, entering and winning competitions. I learned to play Contract Bridge and how to do the Times crossword. I sang in the choir, the choral society and the octet, I was house musical representative, organising the house choir, the choir and singing the solo myself in the inter-house musical competitions. I also acted in various plays. (Bully for me!)

SO WHAT?

So, not only did I become a more accomplished person, I also was given responsibility, in various different fields at a young age. I had to work with, organise and train others. It also shows I was physically fit and could be smart, presentable and disciplined.

These are all qualities that university admissions tutors seek in an individual. Or should.

The last thing they want to discover is that there is nothing to discover about your students. If they are boring, if they never do anything, if they never take any responsibility for anything or anyone, if they have no organisational skills, or cannot demonstrate the ability to think on their feet, then why will they think of giving them a place? All other things being equal.

I do know that there are admissions tutors who look at the predicted grades and nothing else. They don't care presumably about what will be sat in front of them for the next 3 years. Perhaps they are geeks and all they want is other geeks to lecture their geeky subject at. Fine, hopefully your students will get the grades they need and stop worrying. They can spend all their time staring at a screen or playing computer games. But can they take that risk?

My advice is to urge them, if they are not already doing so, to try and find some form of pastime, hobby or sport that allows them to gain some of these qualities while at the same time having fun. Tell them to remember, the private school kids will be doing that anyway and all around the country they will be up against other invisible "enemies" trying to outdo them in all this.

The key thing is to be active not passive, to be creative where that is a good idea, organisational where that will help, to show caring attitudes, to take responsibility where possible.

(More on the UCAS personal statement in another chapter).

Another thing they really must do, if only to be prepared for university interviews, is to keep up with what is loftily called "current affairs". (Believe it or not I actually had weekly lessons on this in prep school.)

Show them that all it means is that they should be aware of what is going on in the world of politics, economics and current events both in the UK and around the world. They may feel this doesn't concern them, but a/ it does b/ they may find themselves surprised at how much they actually find to interest them and indeed they may end up believing passionately in a cause, that they have found out about from following events. It may well come up at interview so they must not appear clueless.

The easiest thing to do is to read a decent newspaper at least once a week. Or to listen to the Today programme on Radio 4, and/or PM. They must not rely on just watching the 6 o'clock news on the TV. ("Jive Bunny's guide to the news"). Tell them that it only ever scratches the surface of what is going on. Explain to them that, whatever "Hello" magazine, Twitter or some Facebook page thinks is important is NOT what a university interviewer will care about.

The Times, the Independent, the Guardian even the Telegraph all bear scrutiny. There are right wing and (all too few) left wing newspapers. They need to try to strike a balance.

The last thing they want to do is end up spouting propaganda they have read in a paper as if it were gospel and the only way of looking at a problem. Explain to them that that will not get them where they want to be, in fact the opposite. That they need to have balanced opinions if they are to impress as mature young adults.

Probably not being readers of the press, they may need to be told how to tell the difference between unbiased reporting and biased comment. Once upon a time the two never even appeared on the same page but nowadays they are often next to one another.

If they want to watch decent current affairs programmes on the TV or via their computer then you could point them towards Panorama, Channel 4 news, Dispatches, and Newsnight. Although you may feel there are others you favour, if so explain to them what they are and why they are so good.

We do appreciate that to them politics may be just dead boring. They may feel "Why bother?" and to a large extent I do sympathize. But remind them that they will be old enough to vote when they are 18 and as the 2017 general election showed, often the young voter can really change things. Explain about how it was in part down to the young voter that the Conservatives lost their overall majority, and if they are voting, they do need to know what they are voting about.

One last thing. Try to help them see that they should not let their free time damage their health. They should "Be wise". (See "How a Healthy lifestyle affects the chances of success.")

13. What they should do about paid employment.

We all know that once they get to 16 or so, paid employment beckons. Many employers know this too.

They want to do it for the obvious reason, to earn some money. There are other less obvious reasons, but they need to be made aware that 2 years' part time work at their local supermarket is not going to sway an Oxford college towards giving them a place reading PPE!

The reason for this chapter is to discuss the pros, cons and pitfalls of paid employment while studying for A-levels.

They will have many reasons for earning money. In my school, a car was high on the list of wanted items. Most who did have a car ran respectable, sensible, small hatchbacks, cheap to buy, run and insure. But even the cheapest cars cost a shedload of money one way or another.

Their social life will cost money, some hobbies cost more than others, drinking costs money, meals out, clubbing, all cost money. Clothes, make-up, etc.

The desire to fit in and be on-trend can be expensive.

There is no place for discussing with them how they should be spending their money, but there IS a place for discussing how much time and energy they should be "spending" on earning it.

The officially recognised "best fit" for an A-level student is to work 8 hours per week, to earn money. Surprisingly, working less is not necessarily beneficial! I have no idea why, if I think it is appropriate I will research it and let you know, but the most important thing is for them to realise that working more hours than this is definitely not a good idea.

Some of them, if not most of them, if not from wealthy backgrounds, feel themselves under incredible pressure to earn money. Mostly down to peer group pressure, but I have known quite a few who do it to save up for going to university, which is kind of difficult to argue with.

To help them think about this in an objective way, they need to be aware of the following.

The pressure to make them work more than the eight hours comes generally from two directions: from themselves because of the perceived need to have more money, and from their employers because they form a cheap, flexible and "malleable" part of the workforce.

If they think they need to earn more than they can earn in 8 hours then they really need to try to understand what they are hoping to achieve with these earnings. They need to be very serious with themselves.

As students, they normally do not have to feed themselves, put roofs over their heads, clothe themselves, at least in a basic way, pay for gas, electricity, water rates, all the things that their parent(s) or carer(s) should be providing. (I am aware that there are special cases where this is not the case, I know there are many young people acting as carers for instance). But if they live in a relatively normal household, the money they earn they are generally allowed to keep, no one expects them to go out to work.

So, hard though it may seem to them, if they lost their jobs and could not find another, they would survive! This really needs emphasising. If they think like this they will realise the wisdom of the saying "Trying to earn too many pennies today may harm your chances of earning many pounds tomorrow."

Above all, they must not fall victim to bullying, peer group pressure. If their trainers are not quite the "in thing", or they do not own a variety of designer handbags, or the latest iPhone, the world will not stop spinning round. They need to be helped to understand that they should allow the other idiots to be ruled that way, to not run with the herd.

Once they have their great degrees and their posh, well-paid jobs, they'll be able to buy all the consumer goods they want, if they so desire.

What is a little harder to deal with is the employer who expects them, at the drop of a hat, to work another shift. They may well threaten to cut their hours if they don't, or even threaten them with the sack. This is not doing them any favours, it is the employers using their youth and lack of experience to fill in a gap in their planning. And once they do this regularly, they will expect them to carry on doing it. It can be very insidious, they may well promise to employ them once they have gone to university, in a shop near their place of study for instance.

The threat to do this, or not do this, really is heavy blackmail. Again, as a young person, it can be very difficult to fight this pressure. But they can and if their employer stops being reasonable, then they really do need to rethink the job.

At the very least they should negotiate with the boss. Agree to do the extra shift but only under certain conditions, whatever they like to ask for, extra pay, one shift less the following week, a guaranteed following Saturday off, something like that. In other words, they need to behave like adults.

By not letting them walk all over them, employers will either respect them and treat them better, or they won't and the students will know that they stink as employers and can go and find better ones.

At least, asking them to do more work means they respect the young peoples' ability to do the job. They must use this.

14. How a healthy lifestyle affects the chances of success.

You may wonder what this chapter is doing in this book. Well, this book aims, in a holistic manner, to look at all the different parts of life as a student, and then to aim at helping you get them to a place where they will achieve the sort of success they want.

Health is a conglomeration of lots of things, as you know, but they need to be aware of the effect that good health will have on the outcome of their A-level years.

If they can be persuaded that a healthy body usually contains a healthy mind, then your only battle will be persuading them how to go about maintaining their health.

The biggest problem is that the mind controls what the body does and once they hit 16, their bodies and minds are changing like mad and sometimes they will have a bit of a problem dealing with things.

Puberty is over, for most of them, but that just brings a whole new set of problems. Physically they will not finish developing until they are into their twenties, but mentally they will continue to develop, in all sorts of ways, for a long, long time. The prefrontal cortex of the brain is the last bit to develop. Here is a quote that, although long will help you explain this to them.

> "Understanding the Teen Brain. It doesn't matter how smart teens are or how well they scored on the SAT or ACT. Good judgment isn't something they can excel in, at least not yet. The rational part of a teen's brain isn't fully developed and won't be until age 25 or so. In fact, recent research has found that adult and

teen brains work differently. Adults think with the prefrontal cortex, the brain's rational part. This is the part of the brain that responds to situations with good judgment and an awareness of long-term consequences. Teens process information with the amygdala. This is the emotional part. In teen's brains, the connections between the emotional part of the brain and the decision-making center are still developing—and not necessarily at the same rate. That's why when teens experience overwhelming emotional input, they can't explain later what they were thinking. They weren't thinking as much as they were feeling."

https://www.urmc.rochester.edu/encyclopedia/content.aspx?ContentTypeID=1&ContentID=3051

So there they are.

Their bodies are as strong and full of energy as they ever will be. Emotionally they are discovering love, sex, political thought, etc, full on. And, what a bind, they are expected to get themselves into a good university, all at the same time. Isn't it enough just to pass your driving test?!!! I forgave my students in advance for thinking this.

But, whether they take a year out, whether they apply now and defer their entry, or whether they follow a conventional route and go straight from school to university, this chapter is relevant to anyone who needs to ensure best grades and best application.

To go back to basics, what does your body and mind need to stay healthy? The result really is – moderation in most things and none of some. But the late teens are times when the teenage brain wants to push the teenage body in all sorts of directions, many to excess. And to try new stuff.

The text book answer will not necessarily be what they want to hear. "Don't smoke – anything. Don't drink to excess. Don't have unprotected sex. Get 8 hours sleep a night. Do a reasonable amount of exercise. Don't eat or drink too much fat, or sugar, or caffeine, or..." (the list is endless).

There ARE young people who manage to do all this, more than I ever thought possible, but then there are others who think nothing of drinking to excess on a regular basis, spending all night "partying", living off burgers, never doing any exercise, smoking, taking drugs, etc, etc.

(The price of their new-found freedom.)

They need it making clear that the advantages of a healthy lifestyle are that you look better, you feel better, and you are able to do your job better, even if "your job" is going to classes and working towards good grades.

The disadvantages are that you may feel you are missing out on what other people are doing.

If you are not naturally a "healthy liver" then doing it may well be a bore and leave you with feelings of guilt every time you "fail".

My attitude is to tell them that it is largely up to them what they do. Most of them will do some of it, some of them will do all of it and some of them will do none of it. But it is their choice, you cannot and should not apply too heavy pressure on them over this.

Resentment will not get them on your side. But get them to just ask themselves one question. "How much harm will it do me to live healthily for the 2 years it takes me to get into university?" If they can manage it, and get onto the course they want, the buzz they will get from that will carry them forward on a wave of optimism and they may well find themselves continuing to live healthily.

Even if it doesn't, somewhere along the line they will be able to say to themselves that they CAN do it, and can go back to it when it counts, i.e. when studying for finals.

I have yet to mention bulimia, anorexia etc. These are all things I have experienced as a tutor and, fortunately, there were no fatalities. But one girl who suffered told me that it is worse than being hooked on heroin. I am not a doctor thus not qualified to pontificate on such subjects, but all I can say is that these conditions have deep-rooted causes which are often beyond the scope of simply trying to get into university. The person suffering does not see it as that.

So it is a good idea to tell them that it is up to all of them to take a bit of responsibility for their friends and, if there is one who is looking like they are at risk, to be a bit brave and try to do something about it.

You know as well as any teacher that in all schools there are staff responsible for "safeguarding". And ALL teachers have to know what to do if a student raises their awareness of it. But your students may not really be aware of this so it is worth reminding them.

So, if a friend is not eating normally, to a ridiculous extent, and wearing baggy clothing to hide their thinness, they should TELL a teacher. Tell them the staff will not blow the gaff on them and "dob them in".

Friendships. What effect can they have on health?

Well they can be a distraction, they usually do not get too much in the way of work, but they must try to ensure it does not happen to them too much. Remind them that their real friends would never want to do anything to harm them or their chances of happiness, so if others are trying to "persuade" them to do things that they know will get in the way of their work, then get them to try to suggest alternatives that mean that they still do things together but at times that will suit them better.

15. How to help them obtain work placements or internships that will improve their chances.

It may well be necessary to explain to your students that these are things you need to have done if at all possible. Many degree courses are extremely difficult to get on to without them. (Yet another case of money buying advantage, unfortunately.) Whether they get to do them during school time will vary very much from school to school. But, again, it is a matter of taking control.

My students all organised their own and largely these were very successful. Sometimes a parent or other adult helped out but often they could not.

It needs explaining to them how this happens to students in the private sector. And that of course, a private school student will not do this in term time as their terms are so much shorter, usually.

I used to illustrate the situation with the following imaginary conversation in such a school between two students, let's call them Nigel and Juliana.

You could get one or two of your students to role-play this little sketch with the appropriate yaahry accents, at least they might get a laugh as well as the point!

N: I say, Jules, your old man is in banking isn't he?

J: Oh yah, he's something big in the Hong-Kong National I think. Why?

N: I'm thinking of giving it a whirl after university, any chance of you giving him a bell and asking him to get me a desk there for say 2 weeks next vac?

J: Don't see why not. Any particular office?

N: Foreign exchange sounds fun.

J: Really? Well, if that's what you want, here goes..

Juliana rings her pop, he fixes it, Nigel gets a plum little internship.

End of story.

So what? Well, the sort of parent who can afford to send their offspring to a PS, (I'm fed up of writing private school out all the time), is the sort of person with clout. They have power and position, so the sort of networking you have just read can go on all the time.

This is not so easy if your friends, family and parents and their friends do not move in the same circles. BUT it is not impossible for students to fix these things up for themselves.

They just have to be bold and persistent, use the net, use their phone, write polite letters and follow them up with polite phone calls. If employers cannot give them what they want, then they could try asking them who they think might be able to help out.

They need to rack their brains for distant relatives, for people who may help. Your school may even have a list of destinations of previous Alumni who may be prepared to help.

They must be prepared to go to another part of the country, or even the world, if they possibly can, to get some experience.

A friend of mine worked in an office in Paris for a year before going to university. He ended up a solicitor, but his French was amazing and opened doors for him when applying for jobs working with expats etc.

I have had students doing placements in fashion houses in London before applying to do fashion design at university.

They need to be prepared to think outside the box and to recruit maximum help. What is the worst that can happen when they ask? Only to be told "Sorry, we cannot do that". But they still might know someone who can.

Remind them that the reason for all this is that they will still have a better chance of doing their desired degree if they can prove they have already done a work placement related to it. In fact, as stated earlier, for some degrees, it is more or less mandatory.

16. How to help them make the best University and degree choice.

Having talked so much about Russell Group universities, you may think that this chapter is redundant, but there is more to this than meets the eye. Or at least your tutees' eyes. So you may need to explain to them that firstly it is important that they make their degree choice first.

Sounds barmy, I know, but the number of students I have known who decided, or thought it was more important, to choose the university first, was astounding.

They had all sorts of reasons for this: to be near to home, to save money, was one, which with today's exorbitant fees is understandable. Others wanted the location, like Bath or Edinburgh, or Bournemouth for the legendary nightlife.

Now obviously it may be possible to combine the degree of their choice with the place of their choice, but we are talking here about obtaining the sort of degree from the sort of university that will give them the best start in life. So they may need to be reminded of the following.

They are being asked to decide, at the age of 17 or 18, what career they may possibly be doing when they retire at whatever age it will be, so far away in the future. That is a lifetime away. They only get one lifetime and they do not want to waste a large part of it stuck in a job they are not happy in. I am aware that many of them, even probably most of them, will in fact change jobs and career direction several times, but they do at least want to start off in the right direction.

They may well not know exactly what jobs they want to do once they have earned their degrees, but they must still make sure that they do degrees in subjects that really interest them. THEM, not their family, not their mates, THEM. They will enjoy the work more, they will work harder at it, they will do better in it and it may well interest them sufficiently to want to do further study in it.

Also, once started on the degree, they will find out even more about what sort of jobs they can do with it. There is an enormous choice of degrees available nowadays, and jobs that previously did not need a degree have now become graduate entry only. With nearly 40% applying to university now, that was always going to happen. They need to think widely about their degree choice. To think about what EXACTLY interests them most and then for each one to see if there is a degree he/she can do in precisely that field. If not, they should cast their nets slightly wider and see if there are degrees in slightly different fields that may interest them. If they know what jobs they want to do, they must look on the professional websites to see what degrees are acceptable. Some, e.g. medicine are inevitably narrow, but some like accountancy are amazingly wide.

Many schools will ensure their students attend a UCAS Fair. This is OK, although how much students get from wandering around crowded halls picking up a rucksack full of prospectuses, (that they could get from the website anyway), I am not too sure. They will get the chance to ask questions of people either on a course at each uni, or lecturing there, even the course they want to do, IF THEY ARE EXTREMELY LUCKY. But obviously it would be physically impossible to have representatives of every single degree course in the country, in one place at one time. They also run lectures on writing personal statements, finance, etc. But these again, can be very biased. The students need to be warned of that.

They must not be frightened of emailing questions to the unis, but make sure they do not make a nuisance of themselves, especially if they then want to apply to the course they have been bothering the lecturers about!

Universities all hold open days, it makes absolute sense that students go to these if they possibly can. There is nothing like putting their boots on the ground as it were and talking to students, hopefully, on the course they are thinking of doing. But they must not be disappointed if this does not happen exactly as they hope it will. As with UCAS fairs, it may be impossible to meet students doing the exact course.

If they know, or can meet, a person doing the job they want to do, they must talk to that person to get an idea of what degree they should do. Their insights may well be interesting and not obvious.

Once they have narrowed down choice of degree, they can look at where they can go to do it. They must be told to read the online prospectus for each university that does their degree. It needs explaining to many of them that this can lead to conflict. Probably many different universities will provide the degrees they are looking for. Obviously they should be looking at the Russell Group first, but if their degree is going to be really specialised, then sometimes only one or two universities will do that course. This narrows their choice and, more importantly, means that competition to get onto that course will be hugely harder.

I have had students apply for, and get places on, courses which were only provided by one university in the country. So it is not impossible, but they must be aware of the need for specialist application and of course they must get the grades they require.

But if they are looking to do more common degrees then the choice can be bewildering and other criteria come into the discussion. They could have a read of this, it is a bit old now but is hugely true.

https://www.theguardian.com/higher-education-network/blog/2012/dec/11/student-choice-higher-education

It will point you and them in the right direction.

It does make the point that Student Satisfaction is not the be-all and end-all; in fact a Russell Group university may well not be that hot on it! But it all depends on what they want to do with the degree.

If their prospective employer is looking for a degree from such a university they may well have to put up with it not coming top of the popularity poll. LSE for instance came very near the bottom in a recent poll on "Student Experience" and in the 2017 "Whatuni" Student Choice Awards, of the top 10, only one was in the Russell Group!! (Small sample size).

But then in a recent Times Higher Education Supplement survey, 7 of the top 10 spots went to RG universities. (Which just proves the saying that there are lies, there are damned lies and then there are statistics.)

The National Student Survey is probably the best one to look at if they want a huge sample size but they do have to like looking at spreadsheets!

One thing to bear in mind is that the government has insisted that the top universities make special efforts to give places to students from state schools, so, all things being equal, they already have a built in advantage. This may be the only time in their lives that coming from an ordinary state school is an advantage, so they should use it!

Above all, they must not allow themselves to be influenced by peer group pressure into making the wrong decision. The decision is for them to make and for them to live with.

17. The importance of making an early UCAS application.

The UCAS application, hugely important as it is, is still something that some students leave until the last minute. Even those who normally can be relied on to hand in work on time and otherwise to be responsible, make this mistake.

The importance of early application needs explaining to them.

Firstly, there are subjects like Medicine, which HAVE to be applied for early, so they need to find out as soon as possible if the subject(s) they are applying for come into this category. This they cannot make a mistake over. I am sure you know this already but they may not.

Secondly, they must be told that there are other tests they may have to take, especially for the top subjects at the top unis. For PPE at Oxford for example, they have to take a Thinking Skills Assessment in early November. It is no good finding this out too late.

As I keep on saying, they have to be proactive and to act early.

Thirdly, it needs explaining that university courses and their admissions tutors fall into two types. Ones where the admissions tutor is a "filler" and ones where he/she is a "chooser". And ALL universities have both types of course, to a greater or lesser extent.

"Fillers" work filling up the empty places on their, not terribly popular, courses. They are desperate to get bums on seats and if they do not get enough takers their course might even be closed down and they might even lose their job. These tutors will take almost anybody who has a fair chance of finishing the degree. Therefore, fair predicted grades, and no evidence of your being a mad-axe-killer, are about all they need to make an offer. But there are vicious cuts going on in Higher Education at the moment so these types of courses are becoming fewer and fewer.

The "choosers" are the tutors who know they are going to fill their courses and therefore care deeply about getting the best possible applicants, to ensure they get the best level of degrees. They have their own inspections, after all. But do they care? Unfortunately, human nature being what it is, some admissions tutors in this enviable position, can still be lazy. They look through applications as they arrive, choose the best ones as they come in, and then make offers until their places are filled up. I know this is unfair and they should wait for the deadline before making their choices, but believe me they don't, not all of them.

How do I know this? Because for years I would ask my year 13 tutor group, every morning: "Who has had an offer?" Not too long after UCAS started processing applications, universities started making offers. Even "unconditional" offers. By rights none of them should have done it until after the closing date.

SO IF THEY WANT TO BE SURE OF A PLACE THEY MUST GET THEIR APPLICATIONS IN WELL BEFORE THE DEADLINE.

Simply getting their applications in early says much that is positive about them. For example, it says they are organised, forward thinking, and once on a university course, are likely to hand work in on time! This, on its own, will make the admissions tutor feel positive towards them.

They need to bear in mind that those desperate "fillers" are waiting in some trepidation for students to accept their offers. They do not want the panic of waiting for "clearing". They do not want to be obliged to fill their empty places with gormless idiots with poor grades and no real commitment.

They need to know just how picky "Choosers" can be. They are looking for the mature, all-singing, all-dancing, super-students. A former Head of Sixth I worked with once spoke about an experience he had had. He visited a friend whose father was the admissions tutor for a prestigious, but not the top, medical school. As he was waiting for his mate to get ready, he realised this chap was going through UCAS applications. He had two piles, one enormous one of rejections and one thin one which consisted of those to whom he was going to make offers. He asked if he could look at the rejections, and while looking through them he noticed one applicant was a straight A candidate, Head Boy, captain of the rugby team, the whole nine yards. So he asked why the candidate had been rejected. (He could not see anything wrong with the application at all.) The bloke then just gave him a withering look and said, "He can't spell "badminton"! Sure enough, he had spelled it "badmington". That was all it took to get rejected.

Let your tutees know that, at this level, the admissions tutors are not looking for reasons to accept people; the applicants are of such calibre that they are looking for reasons to reject them.

I think it is the enormity of the task and its importance, which leads to a certain inertia and unwillingness to take such a huge step. But like all major tasks, it is accomplished by breaking it down into a set of smaller, easily doable tasks.

Explain to them that some of the form is really boring and just pure administration, part of it is the famous Personal Statement, to which I have devoted a separate chapter and some of it relies on others, namely you and their teachers, for their references and predicted grades and you as their tutor for your input into the form. (They may not be aware that everything that staff write is finally amalgamated into one straight piece of prose.) So they also need to be on the ball.

In a sensible school, the staff will have done their input by the end of the summer term in your year 12. There then follows a period of time in which they can modify their reference and, importantly, the predicted grade.

Just a word on grades. It must be made crystal clear to them not to think they can always persuade a teacher to give them a better predicted grade. They must understand that it is not enough to just say, no matter how earnestly, "But I need a predicted B to get into Nottingham" (or whatever). If the school or college wants to be taken seriously by the top universities then it cannot go around over-predicting their students' grades. Too optimistic a grade, in the end, backfires because the universities start to get to know which schools (and even which departments') grade predictions are not to be trusted. The last thing they need is to have an A predicted, which they subsequently obtain, but for the university they are applying to, to think, "Oh no, not them, a D is more like it." And then to not make them an offer.

Every year, schools over-predict grades, it has become expected, but that does not make it better and in the end it just does harm. So, far better to do the work that will persuade their teacher(s) that they really will get a top grade that can then be predicted with confidence.

So, they must get all the admin business done straight away, it not being as straightforward as they might think. They must not think it is easy and can be left to the last minute, it must not.

Tough one this, for you, but if possible try to ensure the staff members with input to the form get their bit done early. If they are not cooperative, apply pressure in the nicest possible way, and if that does not work, get the Head of Sixth to apply the pressure. (I have never had a member of staff be awkward but I have to imagine every eventuality.) Finally they must get the Personal Statement done properly, bearing in mind that if they are doing it early, you and any other people who will need to go through it with them, will not be too busy. As the deadline approaches, staff will be overwhelmed with the statements from all the last-minute-merchants. So earliness brings the advantage of removing pressure from not only the students but also those whom they need to help them.

More on this in the chapter on Personal Statements, but your students must not forget it is unlikely to fit on the form first time. The character count they give you is not accurate, quite surprisingly so.

I hope you have helpful staff, but do give them a chance.

So to sum up:

Get on it early

Get all other tests in motion early

Remember the advantages of being ahead of the crowd

Get staff to cooperate and help you with it early.

18. How to help them write their best personal statement.

I apologise in advance to all the experienced tutors who have been doing this for years. If this is the case then this chapter may not reveal anything new to you, although I think it is worth at least skimming through to ensure you have not got too set in your ways! But please remember I am writing this for tutors of all types including brand new ones.

So here goes with my advice to be passed on to your probably quite apprehensive tutees, as to how to deal with this important piece of writing.

Try not to frighten your students but gently explain to them that this document could well be the most important thing they ever write in their lives. Why? Because it is the only thing, apart from the reference section of the application, that will give university staff an idea of what they are like and thus give them the opportunity to "sell themselves" albeit as subtly as possible.

Without a good degree from a top university, even a good job application letter will not be enough to secure a good job. So this is more important than any job application.

And they want THIS degree from THIS university. Nothing else will do! This is why they need all the help they can get with it.

THEY will be writing it. But they can take advice from whomsoever they wish. Mainly you.

To do a good job, they need to be really organised, to have already performed certain tasks, done certain things, and to have certain qualifications under their belts.

No two personal statements are the same, or if they were then they would show incredible lack of imagination. And they will be caught if this is the case, (see below!) They will find websites which say they can help them, but they need to be very careful of taking their advice too literally and above all they absolutely must not copy parts of someone else's statement, even an example one. UCAS has very sophisticated anti-plagiarising software. They use it to check applications; they say so on their website. So their statements must be all their own work. In this IT technological age, temptation is terrible and they really need to be warned about this.

The best website is the UCAS one itself.

https://www.ucas.com/undergraduate/applying-university/how-write-ucas-undergraduate-personal-statement

It gives far more accurate info than I have space for.

They need to be honest, so it is better that a student actually IS an interesting, committed, responsible person, rather than just to SAY they are. They must be able to prove it. So sentences that contain this sort of thing must also contain examples of this skill or whatever.

They need to know that at interview, the university staff will be hugely experienced and will be able to tell if they are making it all up, within seconds. It is not worth the risk. They need to be able to prove the qualities they say they have. They should start off with a very clear statement as to why they are applying for the course. This must show real interest, real commitment, and some decent knowledge of the subject.

Explain to them that "I want to earn a ton of money" is a crass reason; they need to show passion for a subject as well as an interest in a career that follows on from it.

They must have read the course descriptions in the universities' websites. These will contain the qualities, skills and experiences that it would be a good idea to have before applying.

They need to make very clear what it is that interests them about the subject, and why.

It is commonly thought that the opening sentence makes or breaks the application. (Many applicants look to relate some "epiphany moment" that started them off on the path of studying the subject for which they are applying.) While this is probably an exaggeration, there is no doubt that it sets the tone for it and subconsciously affects the mood of the reader.

Each of them is only making one application, but admissions tutors read hundreds if not thousands of them. If the opening is banal then that is going to put admissions tutors in the frame of mind of expecting a banal application from a banal student. They may not even read to the end of it. (They will be skim reading anyway).

Unless of course theirs is one of the few first applications, as they have taken your advice about applying early! Yet another benefit of applying early!

Talking of hackneyed, here is a list of the most overused opening sentences that you can amuse them with:

1. From a young age I have (always) been [interested in/fascinated by]... (used 1,779 times)

2. For as long as I can remember I have... (used 1,451 times)

3. I am applying for this course because... (used 1,370 times)

4. I have always been interested in... (used 927 times)

5. Throughout my life I have always enjoyed... (used 310 times)

6. Reflecting on my educational experiences... (used 257 times)

7. Nursing is a very challenging and demanding [career/profession/course]... (used 211 times)

8. Academically, I have always been... (used 168 times)

9. I have always wanted to pursue a career in... (used 160 times)

10. I have always been passionate about… (used 160 times)

11. Education is the most powerful weapon which you can use to change the world… (used 148 times)

You'll find all this in the UCAS site. They have to be aware that it will be almost impossible to be totally original in their approach and they need to tread carefully to avoid clichéd prose.

My mother truly did know that she wanted to become a doctor from the age of five, but she was rare.

Admissions tutors live in the real world, so they can be honest, providing of course that such honesty does their application no harm. They should also beware of making their opening statement so blindingly good that the rest of the statement pales in comparison with it, like the opening to Smoke on the Water by Deep Purple, it IS brilliant but the rest of the number does not quite live up to it, does it?

They must tailor what they write to the course for which they are applying. They should find out the sort of qualities that are important when doing the job, if they are applying for a vocational course, such as Dentistry. They must ensure they have these qualities and ensure they can prove this and put that in.

They should refer in detail to the work placement they have done in this, or a related field. Nothing says they are the right person for the course more than having actually experienced the work.

They need to mention their ambition(s). Unless they have ambitions beyond the degree, the admissions staff will wonder why they want to do the degree.

If they are applying for non-directly vocational degrees, they need to think about the sort of qualities that the course will require. Is this creativity, manual dexterity, a good sense of business, good numerical ability, organisational ability, problem solving, the ability to empathise, or something else? (See the universities' websites).

Whatever skills and abilities are required; they will need to be sure they are aware of them, possess them and can prove that with concrete examples of what they have done.

They must comment on parts of their studies that they found interesting, in detail, giving clear reasons why they found them interesting. They must link them to the courses they wish to follow.

They must remember their reasons for applying to the course.

If they are applying for a real mixture of courses, they need to stick to mentioning the skills that they will all require, such as problem solving.

They must refer to their study skills. If they have applied what is in this book, this should be no trouble but they must remember, admissions staff do not know them from Adam, or Eve, so they do need to tell them in some detail the sort of learning strategies they employ.

Personal qualities, to do with their studies, are important. This is rather an embarrassing thing to be writing about. They can say, "I am a hard-working and committed student" but they have to say to themselves, "What can I include to prove this?" Or "Will my teachers all say this about me?" You will be aware that their positive qualities should be made very clear by their teachers. The latter may or may not show the students what they have written, and this decision is one that you cannot advise them on, but they could try saying to you, "Do I need to take up space commenting on this?" Or you could assure them that it is unnecessary, then they can use the space for other things. But the message needs to be put across one way or another.

I did once have a student go to interview at Imperial College who was told that they wanted to find out if all the laudatory remarks made about him in his reference were true! Fortunately, they were and he did his degree there very successfully.

Once they have finished with the academic part they need to give consideration to the part of the statement that shows them as a human being.

Many things have almost universal appeal. Playing a sport or some other physical pastime of some kind is always good. If they have captained a team or organised a championship, or coached youngsters, all that is great stuff. If they have been in the CCF, the ATC, the scouts, the guides or a similar organisation these again are generally seen as being a good thing. They prove that the students can follow instructions, can take care of themselves in various environments, can problem solve, manage others, look after equipment and their appearance and above all that they have some spirit of adventure. Duke of Edinburgh, ASDAN, Young Enterprise, Higher Education Taster courses, all of these will provide a good picture of what they have been doing.

Membership of any group of like-minded people doing some joint activity shows that they can get on with others, bearing in mind that it is very rare to find a job where they will not end up working with others.

If they have a hobby they are passionate about then they can mention that, but do try to make sure it is something adult, not collecting matchboxes or anything like that.

If they have had a "Saturday" job, then they may mention it, as it shows they at least have the gumption to carry out paid employment but they mustn't bang on about it or try to use it as proof that they will win "The Apprentice". If they are really desperate to prove they are responsible then they can use it for that but they must not try to make a silk purse out of a sow's ear.

Work placement or work experience is a totally different kettle of fish.

Other stuff like, "I like reading and doing puzzles". Well, get them to look at it. Does that sound like the most intelligent of 18 year olds? If it matters, and they can say something interesting, then by all means they can put it in, but it must be clear, detailed and to the point. "I generally manage to do the Times crossword in about 45 minutes" is a hell of an achievement. (Moreover, it is unlikely to be put to the test at interview!) And if they are applying to read English Literature then obviously, they are going to mention works they have read and to comment on them in some detail. However, they must not try to pad out a thin application with boring inanities. They will do more harm than good.

If all this means they need to take up a new hobby, then ask them "Why not do so?" They do not all cost the earth and there is usually some voluntary work they can do, which will get them a few Brownie points.

One thing they must avoid is overfilling their personal statement with jargon, in the desire to impress the reader with the idea that they really know what they are talking about. I once had a personal statement from a girl applying to do something to do with fashion that was so full of jargon that I almost could not understand it. I had to keep sending it back to her repeatedly until she toned it down to the point where it flowed naturally and allowed some of her lovely personality to shine through. Once it got to that point, she sent it off and got bang on to the course she wanted, of which there was only one in the country, at a Russell Group university. Rereading it and rewriting it was hard work, but it was worth it. (UCAS also comment on this in their website.)

I once had a heck of a battle with a lad who was applying for medicine and wanted to spell the verb "to practise" as in "to practise medicine" with a "c" as in "best practice". He fought me every inch of the way, even finding some daft doctor to say that THAT spelling was OK. Well it may be in the USA, but not in the UK. In the end he agreed and did fine. (Remember "badmington"?) Impress upon them that spelling, grammar and punctuation really matter, also the more succinct the prose is, the less space it will take up and therefore the more they will be able to get over.

It will also read better, as if written by a brighter person. That is why I have been known to go through some students' UCAS personal statements up to seven, eight, nine times. I even had students from other tutor groups asking me to look at their forms. A bit of a cheek, to be sure, but when I asked them "Why?" They simply said, "We heard you were good at it". So this part of your role is absolutely crucial.

A word about humour. They mustn't! They cannot be sure that their application will be read by a person as young and hip as themselves. It could well be a grouchy, humourless, old fogey. Also they need to avoid religion and politics. You may be surprised at my mentioning this, but I have had students who were so into their faith(s) that they felt it was important to bang on about it in their personal statement. It was not too difficult to help them to change it. I simply made them think about a scenario where the admissions tutor was of a completely different faith or an atheist, or of opposing political leanings.

When writing their statement, they will be told the number of characters they can use, including spaces. 4000 characters in 47 lines, but they must be aware that not all word-processing software counts characters, such as line returns or paragraphs, the same. The only way they will find this out is when they copy and paste it into the UCAS form on the website. So they must do this <u>well before</u> they want to send it off. Nothing is worse than thinking they have pared it down to exactly the right length, still including everything they wanted to put in, (there never seems to be enough characters to do this) to only find, right at the end, that it is still too long. Gutting it is, so forewarned is forearmed.

On the UCAS website, they can do this as they write it, this is enormously helpful, but they MUST remember to save it regularly to stop it shutting down on them. **I most strongly advise** you to advise them to write it directly onto the UCAS website. It really is the best way. Do not make the mistake of assuming that they realise the idea is to write their statement in Word first then copy and paste it into the form.

If they use an Apple, then please take advice as I have no idea! But it is easier to use the UCAS website.

19. How to help them revise effectively, prepare well for exams and make best use of Past Papers.

Ask your students, "Hands up, how many people love revision?" They can then all put their hands down, all none of them!

I do not know anyone who enjoys revision. And what makes it worse is that revision time can coincide with time they would far rather spend doing something else.

As teachers, I and my colleagues dreaded results day if during Easter, and/or the weeks before the exams, the weather had been fine. I taught near a seaside town, and if the weather was remotely decent, many of the students would head off to the beach "to revise". As a friend of mine used to say, "Sure bananas".

Revision can be unbearably boring. And as soon as it is boring people will do anything to avoid it.

A teacher can teach a class of students but they cannot supervise a group of students, at home, who are supposed to be revising.

Some teachers are very clever. At prep school I had a History teacher who went through the whole syllabus, the year before exam year, and then he went through it again in exam year. This was the gentlest and nicest way of revising I can ever remember a teacher doing. And I did well in the History part of my scholarship exam. So it worked. But most teachers are not sufficiently organised, or simply do not have the time to go through the whole syllabus twice. I never did.

Some teachers will have a revision programme and/or run revision classes. I take my hat off to all those teachers who do run these classes. I never did because I felt that there were two problems with them. Firstly, the students were not obliged to go to these classes, so the only ones who went were the sort of students who would have revised sensibly anyway. The idiots stayed away and went to the beach! And secondly, I felt that some staff did them for the wrong, personal reasons. You will have your own view on this and may well disagree with mine. I am sure I am just a little cynical here.

Revision programmes again suffer with the problem that only the conscientious students will follow them. But at least they all had that chance. I dutifully produced revision programmes for my students and all those who followed them did very well.

Here is the point at which they need to be made to realise that they are that sort of student and they will do really well in exams if they attend all revision classes and follow all revision programmes to the letter. BUT it depends on having teachers who will do this for them. The best schools will, but the worst will not.

Whatever their situation, they need to think about exactly what revision is designed to do. This needs to be broken down into bite-sized chunks for them, rather as learning was.

Revision is in fact not one thing but a series of things.

Firstly it is the opportunity to fill in any gaps in notes, and therefore in knowledge. If they have been following this programme then there should not be any of these as the syllabi will tell them what areas of study they should have covered. But there are always the cases where your student may have missed a series of lessons through illness etc., which meant that there were gaps. So their first task is to fill these in, to check that notes are complete and that they UNDERSTAND everything they have to revise.

If there are still points in their notes they do not understand, they must reread the section in the relevant chapter on "How to get the grades".

Secondly, do not let them fall into the trap of feeling that they have to spend equal amounts of time on all parts of the syllabus. If they know a part of the syllabus brilliantly and can answer any question on it without hesitation, then they obviously love it and DO NOT NEED TO WASTE TIME REVISING IT. Doing that would simply be self-flattery, and they do not have the time for that.

Instead, they need to bone up on the areas where their knowledge is more shaky. But they must still make sure they have a good look at ones they are good at to ensure they really do know them well.

Once they are sure that they have full notes on every topic in the syllabus, and understand them, then revision moves into phase two.

Phase two is where they consolidate their knowledge, where they make sure that their recall of everything is faultless and quick. I already mentioned in "How to get the grades" various techniques for recalling the facts that needed for the exam. They must ensure that they use all of these and any others that work for them, to help them recall accurately everything they need.

When doing this, they must try to spend limited amounts of time on this. 45 minutes at a time is a good period to spend on it. It has been proven that students recall well what they revise at the beginning of a revision period, but also that which they revise leading up to a break. So it is obvious that having breaks helps. If they simply sit down and say to themselves, "I am going to revise this until it all sinks in." Then they are heading for a negative experience and one which will not be good revision.

If they absolutely feel they cannot do this, or feel they are doing it but STILL nothing is sinking in, then they need to move straight to phase three, after giving it a decent chance. Tell them not to take this as permission from you to just skip it anyway!

Phase three, active revision. This is where it all comes together and they are really working actively towards exam success. As I said before, nothing works better than actually producing the goods. Here is just one example of what they can be doing. They should look at a past paper question, think about how long they will need to answer the question. Then they should close all books and put them somewhere where they will not be able to get at them easily, like under their mother's legs on the sofa where she is watching television! (Joke, but some of them will be awful cheats!) Then they must use a clock or watch to time themselves and write out the answer. Once they have done that they must use the mark scheme to mark themselves. It must be impressed upon them that they must not cheat here either. If they forgot something they must not pretend that it'll be OK on the day of the exam. It will not. With exam pressure it will be even more likely to happen. They must see what they got right and what they got wrong. Then ONLY WORK ON WHAT THEY GOT WRONG. (i.e. back to phase 2).

The All Blacks coach was once asked how it was that such a tiny community (New Zealand to those of you not up in rugby) could produce such world class players and win so many prestigious titles. He simply replied "We only work on what we are bad at."

What they MUST do is iron out any problem areas, the bits they are a bit scared of, a bit less confident in. By making sure that they can answer any question that the exam board might fire at them, they will really be able to go into the exam room calmly, and quietly confident of doing well.

Past Paper practice is absolutely essential. Their teachers should do this with them. But, lessons being what they are, teachers may well not really put them in exam conditions. They will feel bad about simply sitting there supervising in silence, they will feel they are not doing their job. Their job is to <u>teach</u>, they think. But in fact they should be putting their students in exam conditions. No talk, time limits, no interruptions. And of course, no notes.

Once the question has had its time allocation, they should take the papers in, pass them around the class and the students should all mark each other's from the mark scheme. They will gain far more from this than simply marking their own paper. They will get used to having to put their ideas down clearly so that anyone can understand them. They will have to use clear handwriting. They will have to be succinct and stick to answering the question. When marking someone else's work, they will have questions as to what is an acceptable answer. This they will discuss with the teacher and the whole class. Explain to them that this, when it happens at exam boards, is called "moderation" and it can be very contentious. No two markers see answers always the same way. But they have to do it to ensure that in the actual exam, their answer could not be more clear.

But away from the classroom, they should be doing Past Papers on their own. Being as strict with themselves as they know they have to be and LEARNING from their mistakes. Once they can do entire papers, in time limits, and still score A* according to the mark scheme, then they know they will be OK in the actual exam.

Explain to them that during revision periods, they must ensure that they have a proper timetable and that they stick to it. They should build in periods where they do normal, enjoyable stuff, they do not have to be revising 24/7. In fact that is very counter-productive. They should do what needs to be done but not feel guilty if they have a bit of time off. But they must make sure that they do all they need to do.

20. What to do when their teacher is not up to the job.

This may sound contentious or even downright insulting, but I am putting this in because quite a few of my students found themselves in this situation.

First off, remember that the last thing you want to do is to get yourself involved in questions of unprofessional behaviour. BUT, this happens, more often than OFSTED would like.

Your students may well come to you with this sort of problem and you can deal with it, but it takes tact, diplomacy and a bit of street-smarts.

First of all ensure that they are doing all that they should be doing and that the problem is not with them. And it is not enough for them to agree on the problem with even a large number of members of the same class. They may all be right but I have known of cases where nearly the whole class had chosen the wrong A-level and simply were unaware of the difficulty level of the subject matter. They all, except one, had really low predicted grades.

You know as well as I do, but they may not, that their teachers will have predicted grades for all their students at the beginning of the year. They will find these a little bit weird sometimes. (Tell them to Google "ALIS predicted grade" if they want to find out how these grades are arrived at.) Tell them that this grade should not be regarded as the Holy Grail. They are never 100% accurate, but they are a reasonable indicator of minimum target grade. If their predicted grades for this subject are low then this may in fact be at the root of the problem. They are finding it hard-going and this is not therefore necessarily the fault of the teacher.

Many students read these and get very depressed or upset by them. Being based on GCSE performance, if the student did not work hard for these, then the ALIS grades will be wrong, provided they are now working much harder. But if they really did their best at GCSE, then they may well be an accurate indicator. If their predicted grade for their chosen subject is really low then they have to take a deep breath and think hard about how much they care about, or want to do, this A-level. (See chapter on A-level choice.)

If their predicted grade is good, the problem may be due to a number of factors. Knowing what these are, in itself, will not solve the problem but may lead to following the right path to find a solution.

Firstly it is increasingly the case that the teacher is not teaching the subject as their first subject. (You will be aware of this but they may not be.) (This very rarely happens in a Public School.)

> (17th May 2016 The Guardian) "As schools struggle to recruit staff, more and more teachers are being asked to take on a subject in which they have little expertise. Sometimes head-teachers have no choice. Department for Education figures show 18% of lessons were taught by teachers without a relevant post-A-level qualification for English baccalaureate subjects in 2014. Things are unlikely to have improved since."

 Quite right, in fact they have got worse. Many teachers are having to teach subjects that they are not terribly comfortable with. In this case it is hardly the teacher's fault. In other cases the teacher may be ill, going through trauma, being bullied, have domestic problems or a whole host of "stuff" going on that makes it difficult for them to cope. (You may well have experienced this.)

The very last thing that is likely is that the teacher is rubbish and just does not care. Explain to them that teachers do not do the job for the money, (right?!), they do it because they want to help young people to learn. Nowadays rubbish teachers get found out really quickly and either go through Capability Procedure, improve (or get chucked out), or get out of teaching all together.

However, if you find yourself in this position, here is what you can advise them to do. It is not easy but after all, they have a right to be taught properly.

They and /or their parent/carer(s) need to talk to the teacher. If that does not work, they must go to the Head of Department. If that does not work, they must go to the Deputy Head (Academic) or the Head-teacher.

Once these people are involved, provided they have a case, the teacher, if he/she has a problem, will be forced to do something about it, or the school will be forced to do something about it.

You can explain what this might entail, such as getting a supply in to cover the member of staff's lessons, or taking steps to ensure the teacher is teaching lessons properly through discussion of lesson plans and observation of lessons.

There comes a point where you have to step back from giving them advice on this. Tell them they must be prepared to accept that the situation may well be one that is not easily solved. It may not be possible, especially with timetabling issues, to move them to another class doing the same subject, if one exists, for instance.

Do strongly emphasise to them that the worst thing they can do is get stroppy in the lesson, or stop going to lessons. That puts them in the wrong and becomes a weapon that can be used against them. It becomes "their" fault.

Other solutions may be taken from the following list, some are easier than others, some may not be possible given their personal circumstances, some will be obvious.

If they can afford it, go for a personal tutor, at least short term or to fill in the gaps in their knowledge .

They could join a study group (see relevant chapter).

They could consider changing an A-level, if it is not their main one, but this will depend on how far into the course they are.

They could consider moving to another school, (I really cannot see you saying this to a student but it still remains a possibility. I have had students in their twenties join my course for this reason. But doing this may be a case of jumping out of the frying pan into the fire.)

But the best solution is simply to become as self-reliant as possible. They can try teaching themselves.

I had to do this for parts of two of my A-levels, (yes, at a Public School!) it worked.

By following all the advice given in the chapter on study skills they may well find that any incompetence in the teacher can be compensated for. Also, if it is obvious to the teacher that they really are working hard at his/her subject, it might just be enough to get him/her to admit to the problem and to seek help. The last thing he or she will want is to be in front of a student who seems to know more about the subject than he or she does.

This happened when I was a student at university. The lecturer was forced to mend his ways when we students complained that we were learning more from fellow students when they presented seminar papers than from his lectures.

21. How to help them when they feel low.

I know that most of what I have written in this book seems to imply that once they are on the programme, as it were, everything is going to go swimmingly and they will end up happy as sandboys, in the university of their choice doing the courses they always wanted to do.

But I know that is naïve, there will be times when that does not happen at all, times when they feel overwhelmed and honestly do not feel that they are cut out for what they are trying to achieve. At these moments the world seems to be closing in on them and they do not know where to turn.

That is fine. That is NORMAL. They do not need to feel that all is lost. They just need to come to a point where they realise that their feelings are temporary and they will come to an end.

Do not expect any student to tell you, personally, that they are having this sort of problem. That is most unlikely, no matter how good your relationship might be with them.

So, you need to address the group as a whole and give them the "If this ever happens to you..." scenario. Tell them they **will** (sooner or later) get back to normal and sort out their problems.

Here are the steps to take if they feel they cannot cope or are beginning not to cope:

The first thing they must do is to stop thinking in terms of the big picture. They must not think that their world is going to turn upside down right now. It will not. All they need is the space and the time to sort out whatever the problem is.

Second step, they must ONLY think about what they are going to do for the next 15 minutes. NOT beyond that. Tell them to take a break, go and do something that will take their mind off all the stuff that is in their heads. Walk the dog, or go for a run, or go to bed and sleep.

This is to help them do something that will separate the worrying part of their minds from the events that led up to this crisis. Once they have done that they will gain perspective on the problem.

Perspective means that they will see the problem for what it is, and at the size that it is. It will not be overwhelming. They will start to THINK instead of EMOTE. As soon as they can do that they are on the way to solving the problem.

Reassure them that they are still the brilliant, hard-working and deserving people they always were. That has not changed. They still deserve success and they will still get it. They just need to take the time necessary to solve the problem and then move forward.

There are too many possible problems for me to be able to give you solutions for all of them. They could range from a death in the family to a broken nail. (I am joking about the last one). They will need to find their own solution or solutions.

That is what you have been telling them all along, they know what they need to do. They must **find the solution within themselves**, and talk the possibilities over with responsible people. Their parents, you, their teacher, their Head of Year. <u>Not</u>, you will notice, their mates. These adult people will only want the best for them and will have the maturity to help them reflect in an adult fashion on the problem.

Bullying may be an issue, sadly it often is in schools. Especially if a student has become "different" from the crowd. I can confidently say that my programme with my students in my school had nothing but positive outcomes and none of them got bullied as a result of following it. Maybe the changes are so subtle that others around them will just think of it as their attitude to sixth form study. Maybe I didn't need to write this paragraph at all, but, as I have said before,

I have to imagine all eventualities, and there may well be schools where bullying is rife and this advice is needed. My wife has a friend whose daughter suffered terribly with this, but she just got A*, A, A, all in Russell group preferred subjects, so the problem can be solved!

So here goes. If this happens to them, tell them to try at all times to remember that their <u>real</u> friends know what they are like and would not try to hurt them. Those who try to hurt them are not friends at all, and thus their opinion of them does not matter.

If their old friends cannot take the new them, then it is probably time to move on. People change as they get older and wiser, their real friends will change with them or will just understand that they need to make changes to better themselves and still stick with them.

Whatever the problem, once they have thought coolly about it, the solution will probably be fairly obvious. If it is as big as something like having taken the wrong A-level, then the solution may have to be a bit dramatic, but it will not be the end of the world. If they have to go and do another year of school or college, to do the right mix of A-levels, then that is what they must do.

This is precisely what my grand-daughter had to do, so she only went to university at 20 years old, but she is now doing exactly the course she wants to do.

Really impress upon them that, whatever they do, they must not for a moment think of carrying out some melodramatic act. Anything that causes them harm will not improve the situation. They will suffer, their friends and family will suffer and nothing will end up solved or improved.

Make it clear to them that their brain is a hugely powerful instrument. They must trust it to solve their problems.

22. How to help them write really good essays.

I am sitting here saying to myself, "Do I really need to write a chapter on this?"

Having taught General Studies for years, in the days when all sixth formers did it and a good grade could actually make the difference between getting a place, or not, at one's preferred university, I think I may well have to.

A good teacher should always be able to help them to write a good essay, but do they all? I cannot be certain of this. Some teachers do not think they should do this, maybe some cannot, maybe they teach subjects where essay writing is not a vital part of their skills. So here goes.

Get them all to get a real grip on the following and please, if you are a brilliant essay writer, and have no trouble teaching how to do it, do not feel patronised, but do ensure you teach them how to do it.

Tell then a good essay is absolutely all about preparation and planning.

It is no earthly good getting hold of a sheet of paper, or opening a new Word document, and simply starting to write an essay. Explain that if they do this, their poor old brains are trying to do about 4 tasks at once. Not a good idea.

A Discursive or Expository essay, the type you are normally asked to write, consists of:

Research

Decisions what to include and what to leave out

Marshalling of ideas to argue against and/or defend a proposition

Laying out these ideas in an orderly fashion

An introduction

The body of the essay

A conclusion

All written in good and succinct English, or, if in a foreign language, in good and succinct Portuguese. Or whatever.

The actual writing of the essay should be the simplest part, in which they put down on paper the ideas they have already worked out, and in which all they need to concentrate on is the quality of the language they are using. The French call the essay process, Thesis, Antithesis, Synthesis. This is quite a good way of looking at it. You put forward an idea, you try to shoot it down, then you assemble all the good parts from both sides of the argument to come up with the best solution.

https://www.essay.uk.com/guides/types-of-essay/discursive-essay.php

As long as the above website is available, it gives a good idea of how to do this.

First of all they must ensure absolutely, that they have understood the question or the topic that the essay must deal with.

Secondly, at all times, they must keep looking back to the question and make sure that all they write is relevant to it. They must also keep looking at what they have written and asking themselves "So what?" If the answer to that does not link directly to the question, then it is superfluous.

They must remember, their research is to be done to find arguments and proof of these arguments to back up both the "for" and the "against" side of the argument. They cannot simply make a point because they think it is true, they have to have backing from a third party source. Their "proof" if you like.

So, in the introduction, state clearly the point of the essay, what the argument is going to be about and why it is important. They must not feel they even have to write this before they start. Thanks to the glories of word-processing, they can write the introduction once they have finished the essay if they wish. Whatever they do, they must keep it short and to the point. If writing this essay in an exam, if necessary, they can simply leave space at the top of the first page and write it in at the end. But impress upon them that, for heaven's sake, they must not forget to do it!

In their planning, they should produce a paragraph-by-paragraph plan of the essay. A skeleton if you like, on which they will hang the flesh of the arguments.

Each paragraph must contain the point being made and the proof of the "rightness" of that point of view, that argument.

The body of the essay should be a ping-pong match where they sit as umpire and explain the two sides of the argument. First one point of view is put, backed with some "proof" then the other side contradicts it, with proof of its own, this goes on down the page, with a paragraph for each point, for each side, until about 4 to 6 points have been made.

Each paragraph must not consist purely of comment or what they think but also it must not be purely a quote or quotes from other people's work. There must be a bit of both.

If they really want to make an important point, they will be tempted to hammer it home with lots of quotes. Tell them they do not need to put in more than 3 quotes referring to any one point. No need to use a sledgehammer to crack a nut.

And to remember, if their essay is about a book or a play, they must not simply retell the story. The examiner knows it and does not need to be told it!

Then finally write a conclusion which briefly sums up the points made so far, possibly includes their own conclusions and why they have come to them and then addresses the issue of where the argument can move forward, further research into the subject that needs to be done etc.

They should not try to sum up ALL that has been written in the body of the essay, if they do that they will be rewriting the essay! Pointless!

Finally, after the end of the essay, they should include a reference section in which they list the sources of all quotes. As they enter a quote in the body of the essay, a number should be put at the end of the sentence. At the bottom of the page, or at the end of the essay, the same number should appear next to the author of the quoted work, the title of the work and the date it was written.

In Word go to the "References" tab, then click on "Insert Footnote" and simply use common sense. It is all pretty straight forward.

Put it this way, if the essay includes too few quotes it is a good indicator that not enough research has been done!

23. How to help your students think about how to finance their degree.

This is a hugely daunting part of the whole process of obtaining a degree. For students from working class backgrounds this may well be the make or break question. They will not be keen on taking on the huge debt that a degree incurs.

This is probably the key factor in ensuring that students from middle-class backgrounds are more likely to do a degree than their less well-off friends.

If a student comes from a background where even taking on a mortgage is an impossible dream then the money needed to go to university seems like a nightmare. Getting over this is a huge challenge.

You will need to work really hard to convince some of your students that incurring this debt really is the right thing to do. You will need to make the situation crystal clear to them.

Two aspects of it are absolutely key, firstly that their degree will open the doors to them which will allow them to earn far more than the national average and thus they will be able to repay the loans.

Secondly that the repayments do not start until they can afford them, that they are not big repayments and that if they do not pay off their loans during the expected repayment period, the loan will be written off.

No heavies will be coming round demanding the money with menaces.

Explain to them that there are basically two parts to the costs of a degree. One is the cost of tuition fees, i.e. what the university will be charging to get a degree. The other is the cost of living while a student. The UCAS site gives them some help on this.

There is a tuition fee loan which covers them, at the moment, up to £9,250, which should cover most degrees. They should also expect to get a loan to help with living costs. These will not be expected to be repaid until the degree is finished and the graduate is in employment. Even then, the rest of the repayment will depend on how much they are earning and there is a fixed period during which they will be repaying. If they get to the end of that period and have not repaid it, it is written off.

So finance should not be a limiting factor in relation to applying for a degree. But that is not the end of the story.

There exist other ways of financing a degree which will give them money. There exist bursaries or scholarships which can come from a variety of suppliers, very often from the universities themselves.

If they fancy trying for a bursary or a scholarship, let them have a look at this website:

https://www.thecompleteuniversityguide.co.uk/university-tuition-fees/other-financial-support/university-bursaries-and-scholarships/

This should give them some idea of what is available.

This website:

https://www.thecompleteuniversityguide.co.uk/media/4109415/bursaries_scholarships_grid_england_2017_jan_18.pdf

Very clearly lists the type of bursaries available and what the criteria is for acceptance.

Each of the four countries in the UK has its own grid, they just need to look at them. But they all have the same thing in common, if they make the effort to apply, it is quite possible to lower costs a bit by being aware of these and applying for them.

The main criteria are:

household income, i.e. parents don't earn too much,

where they live, i.e. areas which do not traditionally provide many students,

awards for placement or travel abroad,

awards to disabled,

for excellence in sports,

music,

if they need care,

specified subjects,

and academic awards.

These are awarded to students who are exceptionally bright and/or hardworking who get great results. For example, Reading University was in the papers last week after being criticised for giving scholarships to refugees living in the local area. It said that "...bursaries are automatically offered to UK students from low-income families if they meet the criteria."

Also some unis offer awards to students who basically just make decent progress. This really is not hard to achieve so if they can get one of these, they should go for it, they **really are** painless.

So basically, if they are very bright and/or come from a disadvantaged background and/or are going to study a subject that is pretty rare and unpopular, they may be able to get a scholarship or a bursary.

It is always worth contacting the university to see if anything is available. But they must check out the small print on any offers. It is really important that they understand exactly what the criteria for eligibility are and that they fit them.

Also, they must not let the tail wag the dog. Choice of degree must not only be based on the possibility of a bursary or a scholarship. Tempting though this may be, it is short-sighted if that is all they look at.

They should still be aiming at a degree from a good university. Even the best bursaries are not huge and should not sway them from their absolute goals.

Surviving financially once your students get to university.

These sites could help somewhat.
https://www.savethestudent.org/extra-guides/freshers/13-skills-to-help-you-survive-university.html

https://www.independent.co.uk/money/spend-save/a-students-guide-to-financial-survival-you-dont-have-to-drown-in-debt-at-university-9686930.html

Make it clear that finance is not rocket science. To be financially healthy they simply have to spend no more than they earn or have borrowed through loans, bursaries, grants or scholarships. Or what their parents have given them.

Simple maths means that they can work out their weekly costs of rent, transport, food, energy costs, etc. Once that is done, anything left over is theirs to spend as they wish, and most of them will wish to spend it on nights out.

You probably have sessions on this in your sixth form programme but if not, help them to realise that they need to learn to really keep on top of their budgets by looking really regularly at their banks statement(s) and any other statements they get. They should check out the possibility of any discount card. They should not allow themselves to be caught up in any schemes or to fall for any amazing offers. If it seems too good to be true, IT IS!

They should be prepared to get a job, even if it is just a few hours a week. What I did was to take out of the bank each week what I could afford to spend, in cash, and to never have debit or credit cards on me. That way, once it was gone it was gone, and I never went over budget. Again, tough love but a lesson that is well-learned.

This site lists ten things to look out for that they might not think of when budgeting and also has a useful link.

https://university.which.co.uk/advice/student-finance/student-finance-budgeting-things-to-remember

They will have had friends who will run seriously out of money three or four weeks into term and all you have to say to your students is, "Will they have a much better time over that four week period than you will?" The chances are they won't yet they will be the ones to suffer.

Budgeting seems to be an awfully grown-up pain to have but without it the pain is even worse, and the numbers of students who drop out due to financial troubles is frightening.

Tell them to try not to be one of them.

Conclusion

Hi! If you have got to this point, it means you have read the book.

Not too long was it? I hope you have got something out of it. I hope it did not seem impossible.

Believe me, if you have yet to try following the steps in the book, just take them one at a time. Rome was not built in a day and a really good student does not become one overnight either, but the first step is the hardest.

Once you get started, everything I have said will fall into place and you will find it just becomes part of their lives, and yours.

Remember, many students who have passed through my hands thought at first that some of what I was telling them was either obvious or unnecessary. But after a while they realised that the whole thing is like a jigsaw and if pieces are missing then they do not get the whole picture.

I expect they will look back on their time spent doing GCSE and realise how little actual thought they put into the learning process. How much they entrusted others with their academic achievement. How much they simply did what they were told with little thought of whether the process could be improved.

Warn them that once they start on the process, they should be prepared for their classmates to be a bit surprised by what they know and the questions they ask the teacher. Also by the improvement in their marks! They must not get flustered, they should simply tell their mates why they are doing it and to get hold of a copy of my book for students. After all, they, as classmates, are not in direct competition with each other and the stuff in my book is not a secret, but I would hope that they would be good enough friends to help them get the advantages that they themselves are getting from the knowledge contained within the book, or gained from listening to you.

But if they are shy, they can just shrug and get on with it! I sincerely hope that your students get the places they want in the Universities of their choice.

I do not know you but I have helped lots of students like yours and I hope that many more of them will get the places they want without having to go to Private School first! I also hope that you will enjoy the deep satisfaction that I have enjoyed whenever a student smiles all over their face when they tell you they have got an offer from a great university, or they have got the grades they really needed.

Please look forward to this, and the cards, (and the presents!) from both grateful students and their parents.

I did it, you can do it!

www.ingramcontent.com/pod-product-compliance
Lightning Source LLC
Chambersburg PA
CBHW032038040426
42449CB00007B/937